Climate Change for Beginners
A Primer for Young Minds!

*Exploring the fundamentals of climate change
and its inevitable effects on the food chain, the economy,
culture, and national security.*

Thomas R. Shipley, Ed. D.
December 2019

© December 2019 Thomas R. Shipley, Ed. D.
All rights reserved.
Revised edition.

ISBN: 1732750388
ISBN-13: 9781732750388

Contents

Acknowledgments v

Prologue vii

Preface xi

Introduction xviii

1: Cause and Effect 27

2: Understanding the Basics 37

3: Institutionalized Procrastination 42

4: How Bad Can It Really Be? 50

5: Big Deal #1 - The Food Chain 57

6: Big Deal #2 - Water 77

7: Big Deal #3 - Melting Ice 82

8: A Call for Action 94

9: Final Thoughts 102

About the Graphic Artist 105

About the Author 106

Acknowledgments

Sincere thanks to Pat Swanson and Scott Shipley for their ideas and suggestions in moderating the intensity of my opinionated opening remarks.

A special thanks to my partner, Chris Taylor, for his talent and unwavering patience in word-by-word, line-by-line critique and editing.

*"There is no need for that to be in **bold**...*
You use way too many commas...
Have you verified that statement?
There's no need for uppercase..."

Prologue

Climate change—previously and more accurately referred to as global warming—is *not* some trivial title given to the inconvenience of an unexpected rain storm on the day of your family's picnic. It is *not* about the frustration you feel when a surprise November snowstorm hits on the day you have important travel plans.

*Climate change is
a proven global deterioration
of traditional weather patterns.*

The speed and severity of that change have been unnaturally accelerated and amplified by human interference in every phase of nature's delicate balance. It affects every single thing we do during every single day of our existence.

- Because much of its impact has not hugely touched the lives of the under-informed,
- Because much of it is unseen and therefore plausibly "deniable,"
- Because it has not yet personally effected enough influential legislators, and
- Because most are preoccupied with their day-to-day survival

…we as a people have chosen to ignore the pending crisis. Not a *potential* crisis, a *pending* crisis.

Even though there are millions already directly affected by temperature change, sea rise, droughts, and fires, there remains doubt among many people about the validity of the claim. While they sense no immediate danger, with just a little investigation, they would find three truths:

- Climate change is finally a *well-documented*, academic, scientific, observable, and verifiably reality. (97.1 percent of scientific studies concur.)
- Climate change is directly caused by human interference in nature's balance. (Atmospheric carbon dioxide, one of nature's greenhouse gases, is up 50 percent in the last decade alone. Six of the hottest global years on record occurred between 2014 and 2018. As of this writing, 2019 is on track to be the hottest year yet.)
- Climate change is an immediate threat, an omen of a long-range catastrophe. Habitable and arable dry land, food supply, health, breathable air, potable water, the economy, and national security are all at risk.

How does one make this point strongly enough? The points in this book are not the ramblings of a doomsday preacher pounding on a pulpit to stimulate bigger donations. These are well-documented facts, so serious that the devastation of each point has now begun to feed on themselves. This is causing the problems to grow exponentially and now is outpacing the direst informed predictions. Quoting an article from Chris Mooney in the Washington Post headlined, "New science suggests the ocean could rise more—and faster—than we thought…" on October 26, 2017:

"In one case, the research suggests that previous high-end projections for sea level rise by the year 2100—a little over three feet—could be too low, substituting numbers as high as six feet at the extreme, if the world continues to burn large volumes of fossil fuels throughout the century."

(In more recent sources, I have seen reliable studies estimating that number to be as much as eight to eleven feet.)

*****

It is unclear how much more proof our legislators need.

Perhaps if US House members had been in Moore, Oklahoma in May 2019 to witness the *repeat* of the 2013 EF5 tornado as it destroyed the same town for the second time in six years, they wouldn't be so skeptical.

Perhaps if US Senate members understood that an EF5 tornado with winds of over 200 miles per hour had destroyed a town of 3,000 homes and reduced the landscape to resemble that of Hiroshima, they might talk about something other than the latest "outrage" in the daily news cycle.

Perhaps if our President had helped the search and rescue team to remove the bodies of children from an elementary school there, he would be more thoughtful about who he appointed as Secretary of the Environmental Protection Agency.

Try your best to forget the comfort of where you are right this minute. Instead, imagine a future in which your granddaughter is having a conversation with her three children. She is telling them that they must move because their community on Maryland's Eastern Shore (or Miami, or New York) will soon be underwater. She hides her fear as she explains that she doesn't know where to go because there is no housing available anywhere and she can't find employment. Businesses and industries have closed because of flooding and departing employees, and the region's economy is collapsing. She conceals her anxiety about looming civil unrest.

I invite you to re-think that scenario, and decide for yourself if the involvement necessary to reverse global warming is worth your time and effort.

> While I admit that the climate change we will be discussing
> will only moderately effect *your* existence today,
> (and therefore seemed less than critical,)
> it will, without immediate, drastic intervention
> be devastating to the generations to come.

It's bad enough that we are leaving the next several generations with trillions of dollars in government debts; we have also decided to leave them an uninhabitable earth. Billions are being spent on the science of how to inhabit other planets when we haven't learned how to cohabitate with Mother Nature on this one. Since the Industrial Revolution, we are slowly but methodically smothering her. That money would go a long way toward investigating and developing alternative energy source development—the ultimate solution to the problem.

Preface

Before we get serious, let's just play for a minute or two and set the scene with a light story:

Understanding Extinction

Imagine that one day, several million years ago, old "Ca'put," the Granddaddy Dinosaur, called the herd together and said:

"Well, gang…it's been a great run, but I've noticed that since those volcanos have been fouling up the atmosphere, our weather has been changing something crazy. It's far too cold all the time, and food hasn't been as plentiful as it used to be. I know that we've been hanging on, in spite of everything, but I'm really getting concerned."

"I've tried not to worry y'all with this, but several of us have been down by the river discussing the situation …and the signs are becoming undeniable. Things are changing drastically, and many of us think we are in for some seriously bad times."

Several young Dinos perked up, a very few listened, and the others just smiled. They loved the old guy, but he must be well past a hundred. What does he know?

The uninformed Dinos thought:
"We're young, we're happy, we've been here a long time, and we'll be here forever."

But, Old Ca'put continued:

"Things are much more complicated than just the weather. All the wisdom and all the signs we have experienced in our long lifetime indicate that that strange light we're seeing in the evening sky is probably an incoming asteroid. If its impact with Earth is as catastrophic as we expect it to be, you all may well be the last generation."

Self-Awareness

Of course, this conversation never happened. Never happened because the dinosaurs—like all animals, *except one*—were missing one critical capability, one vital skill. Most animals have no *awareness* of their pending mortality. They were surely not having such a conversation, but rather were just eating, sunning themselves, and perhaps checking out a young tyrannosaurus who just wandered into the valley. They had no idea of what was about to happen. They had no ability or desire to predict the future.

*With no **awareness** <u>they</u> could make no diversionary plan.*

From a poem by Thomas Gray more than 250 years ago comes the phrase, "Ignorance is bliss." Carried a little further, ignorance can also be *comfortable*; it can make life *easy* and an *escape from reality*. How stress-free life must be for those millions who do not understand cause-and-effect relationships, those who don't understand the complexity of their environment, and who naively reassure themselves that "everything's going to be OK."

Now please watch this one carefully: While the saying "ignorance is bliss" is proven to be true time and time again, there is an equally familiar saying that is blatantly false.

"What you don't know won't hurt you."

That statement alone can even be dangerous. If you don't know you have a cancerous tumor, you can't have it removed. If you don't know a train is coming around the bend, you may linger a little too long at the crossing.

*Knowing, yet not reacting to what you know
will surely hurt you.
In the case of climate change and global warming,
inaction may hurt us to the point of eventual annihilation.*

When there is no *awareness*, when there is a *limited understanding* of the complexity of nature, and *when naivety nurtures ignorance*, then one would have no reason to fear the future. When there is no need for deep thoughts or evaluation and when everything is OK, why change? Why get involved?

Everything has been fine for a long time, so surely
everything will continue to be OK.

Imagine further that a few of the dinosaurs *were* paying attention, and some had uncomfortable feelings. They secretly *did* understand old Ca'put's wisdom and warning. What do you think they would be discussing? What panic-driven debates might they be having?

- Would the entire herd eventually come around to believing the old dinosaur?
- What course of action should the informed ones now take?
- Would they be able to separate fact from fiction?
- If they avoid talking about it, would the problem go away?
- Would it help to place blame on a different species over in the next valley?
- Exactly what should they do?
- Is it too late to do anything?

Opposable Thumbs

Humankind is fortunate to have many more superior traits than other animals, more than merely the development of our much-touted opposable thumbs. Possibly the most critical trait is the one that has shaped who and what we are as a species. Can you imagine where we would be without our depth of understanding and *awareness*? An awareness of self, an awareness of our own mortality, and most of all, an enhanced awareness of cause-and-effect relationships?

Some people go through life and, for a variety of reasons, are not taught these things. Some never figure them out for themselves. Far too many simply choose to ignore them.

*****

There are millions of us who do not understand how to effectively evaluate a challenge, to thoughtfully consider all findings, to purposefully respond to those findings, and especially to appreciate the consequences of the cause-and-effect relationships.

Chimpanzees, with their opposing thumbs, understand how to stick a piece of grass into a tiny hole in an anthill and lick the ants off the grass as the ants scurry to investigate the intrusion. Otters understand how to break open a clamshell with a rock to get to the tiny morsel inside. Wolves understand the value of hunting in a pack, surrounding and collectively overpowering a significantly larger prey.

However, none of them really understand why.
They are all operating on instinctive autopilot.
They are operating under basic learned behaviors.
They hunt, they eat, they breed, and they sleep…
that's it!

They cannot think deep thoughts!
They cannot predict the future.

Humans, being the advanced species that we are, do have the ability to think those deep thoughts, to be aware of the cause-and affect behavior, to understand *why,* and to predict the future.
As humans, we have come to a rare crossroads in our long existence. We are about to be tested on that innate ability to use our awareness, to use our understanding of cause-and-effect behavior, and to reflect on—and even shape—the inevitability of our mortality.

What does all this have to do with climate change?

- Animals did not evolve to understand when and why things happen. They only understand that they do.
- Humans, on the other hand, evolved to understand not only when things happen, but also why.

The difference in the success or failure of this test we humans are facing will not be measured in the amount of scientific data we can record or in the volumes of information we can print. There is already an overwhelming collection of compelling data collected and recorded that is easily available. Regurgitating statistics is not the intent of this book.

Everyone knows we have the *intelligence* to evaluate this situation we find ourselves in, and we have the ability to gain *knowledge* from that evaluation. The critical question is, do we have the *wisdom* to use what we have discovered from that evaluation? The test will be passed or failed by our ability to *use the awareness* that only we have.

Today's choice is simple:
Do we have the collective self-discipline
to take the drastic action required by the blatantly evident
path of action
that our intelligent evaluation has prescribed?

– OR –

*Do we pretend that we are not aware of the evidence and,
as lower forms of creatures would tend to do,
assume that everything will continue tomorrow
just as it was yesterday?*

In this book, we will explore many things. None are aimed to solicit a quick response; neither are they written as scientific essays. They are structured as short, common-sense parables to help you understand the seriousness of the situation and to inspire action. They are presented to help you make informed decisions about the gravity of these mounting claims that "the climate is changing," that "the world is warming," and "the sea is rising."

Advocates and critics alike can continue to change their name for the problem we face from *global warming* to *climate change* to perhaps, one day, a new term that's felt to be more nuanced or less off-putting, but they can't change the impact of what's happening.

I invite you to think about the interrelated and unforgiving pieces of this incredibly complicated puzzle. (Please refer to the Spidergram in Chapter 2.) If you are not yet comfortable with such terms as *mandatory evacuation* or *population relocation*, now is the time to learn the depth of their relevance. I invite you to consume, digest, and benefit from our journey through these vignettes.

Introduction

For sixty-five years that I can remember, scientists and prophets, meteorologists and biologists, public school teachers and Ivy League professors have all been belittled and ignored because their cry for action against climate change was, as Al Gore so eloquently put it:

"An inconvenient truth."

Within the next few chapters, we will consider the ramifications of continuing to ignore those truths, no matter how inconvenient. Together, we will reflect on some important facts, the need for some critical decisions, and the urgency for today's young minds to take action. What we do with the concerns expressed in this book will ultimately determine the life or death of the very habitat in which our civilization has developed; the habitat where humans have thrived for eons, and the one in which they and their family had planned to survive. Our planet is in immediate danger. Never before has so much depended on the behavior of the next generation.

The discovery of fire,
the establishment of all the world great religions,
the finding of exotic foreign new lands, and walking on the Moon,
are all as nothing
if we kill the tiny planet on which we exist.

This book was written for young, concerned, inquisitive citizens, especially tweens, high school, and college students. But I'm sure Mother Nature would appreciate all the help she can get from those all who are informed, optimistic, and young at heart.

If this budding group of activists cannot, does not, or will not take the following pages seriously, then far too soon, the *end* of the path we are all on will appear over the horizon. The view will be literally filled with floods and fires of biblical proportion. It is bad enough that this will be frightening and overwhelming to witness, but worst of all, it will by then be irreversible.

Please remember that word as together we explore some ideas. The importance of *irreversible* will become more and more evident as, together, we think through the many ramification of climate change.

Please also remember that right now, some in our government are considering the expenditure of billions of borrowed dollars to put a person on Mars. This astonishing proposal is justified by inflated claims of national security, scientific advances, new jobs, and valuable technical spin-offs. Each of these, when taken separately, contains a grain of truth, but none fully justifies the expense. Similarly, the late brilliant theoretical physicist, Stephen Hawking, recently suggested that it is our "government's *responsibility*" to establish a colony on another planet. While Hawking's motive is different, the folly remains the same.

We, the industrialized population, have contaminated, polluted, and poisoned *this* planet to the point of being increasingly uninhabitable—driving species to extinction. We are now proposing that we should move on to contaminate another. That takes nerve! That takes selfish arrogance! News Flash! Space stations and moon colonies are supplied from Earth.

This book will take you through a nontechnical journey into this many-layered dilemma. Each section, standing alone, reflects a concern. Collectively, they combine to describe a problem more serious than ever before imagined. The overall situation is complicated and difficult to explain briefly. (Remember to study the Spidergram in Chapter 2.)

The purpose here is not to repeat volumes of scientific data. Rather, it is a quick and easy read for those not yet ready to get involved with the solution.

There is already more scientific evidence than you can possibly read. We already know what's causing the problem *and* **we know how to solve it. Neither of those are our problem.**

- We know where the carbon dioxide is coming from, and we refuse to curtail the use of fossil fuels.
- We know what specific steps need to be taken, yet there is no perceived urgency.
- We have not reached the point where the voices of the informed exceed the influence of commercial interests that extract and consume fossil fuels.
- We understand that targeted *population control* is a taboo subject regardless of its validity toward solving the world's problems, so we remain cowardly quiet.
- We understand the dangers of deforestation, but we continue to cut down billions of trees each year. (Note: in our first four hundred years, 90 percent of the United States' old-growth forests have been consumed.)
- As in so many other areas of concern, the blind adoption of Political Correctness stifles constructive conversation.
- Uninformed emotion continues to outshout logic.

This book is a collection of fact-based stories intended to help you think more clearly, understand the gravity of the situation, and connect the dots. I will share facts and conditions, and you can decide if it's something worth your involvement. I hope that you will see the devastating repercussions of *not* getting involved. For instance:

- In the spring of 2017, residents of entire fishing villages in the Dominican Republic, previously on dry land, were moved by their government into public housing on higher ground and their homes were being bulldozed into the mud left by rising seas.
- During that same spring, a paper published in *Nature* by some of the world's top scientists says climate change's effects on what recently was a pristine, productive ocean floor are leading to irreversible changes to the world's coral reefs. The paper urges the government to save the coral reefs so they may continue to maintain their biological balancing functions. (More details of that function will be covered in Chapter 5.)

There are many situations where, in an effort *to do something*, the citizens and their governments are spending billions to solve the wrong problem. Two examples:

1. In 1953, eighteen hundred people lost their lives in an unexpected flood in Rotterdam, the Netherlands. Seventy-two thousand became homeless. Businesses, homes, infrastructure, and farmlands were destroyed or rendered nonproductive for decades. *Forty years later*, the city completed one of the largest and most expensive fabricated efforts ever attempted in an effort to hold back the sea. Massive floodgates, some bigger and heavier than the Eiffel Tower, can now open and close hydraulically. Their goal…their plan…their hope…is to hold back the sea rise up to three meters (roughly ten feet). But note, the flood surge of 1953 was *3.8* meters (about *twelve* feet). Since twelve is greater than ten, where is the logic?

If you are not familiar with the geography of the Netherlands, please take the time to study a map carefully, and try to rationalize the odds of success in preventing sea rise/sea surge ever being adequately prevented by any means, in Rotterdam. After glancing at the map, what do you think about the probability of success?

2. In 2005, New Orleans and large areas of the United States Gulf Coast were devastated by Hurricane Katrina and its resulting floods. Again, over eighteen hundred people lost their lives, and damage was measured in the billions of dollars. The US Army Corps of Engineers, Louisiana citizens, and several US government agencies involved agreed to build and install the "world's largest" array of pumping stations, supported by huge surge protection barriers *and*, yet another hydraulic floodgate system.

Make no mistake. These catastrophes are the result of unusually severe weather conditions and are not entirely or solely related to global warming trends. However, they *are* indicators of the devastation caused when water invades our habitat. They are also examples of how the people and their governments fail to respond properly to similar crises.

*****

The *original* problem with the New Orleans dilemma was the conceit of the people who thought they could outsmart the fundamental nature of a floodplain. They thought that they could stop nature from the inevitable. This elementary (and exaggerated for clarity) cross-section might have suggested to the early city planners that this is not a good place to start a town.

Climate change was not the only cause of recent flooding there, but it is implicated in recent patterns of extreme weather events. Most scientists agree that there's an undeniable relationship and an exponential growth in both.

*It is difficult not to smile—just a little—
at the well-worn axiom,
"Mother Nature bats last ..."*

Given increasing weather extremes, such flooding is going to become more commonplace across the world each year with even more devastating results. The installation of physical and mechanical barriers is barely a short-term answer! Every concerned citizen must help elected representatives understand that the billions of dollars now being (mis)spent in this way must be redirected to more realistic and longer-lasting solutions.

Fifty percent of the Dutch population now lives below sea level. They live in fear of devastating floods, and they spend massively to compensate for the expectations of advancing water and weather extremes. What follows is elementary logic:

- As any body of water warms, as the air above it warms, more water evaporates, which rises into the air more easily and with more speed.

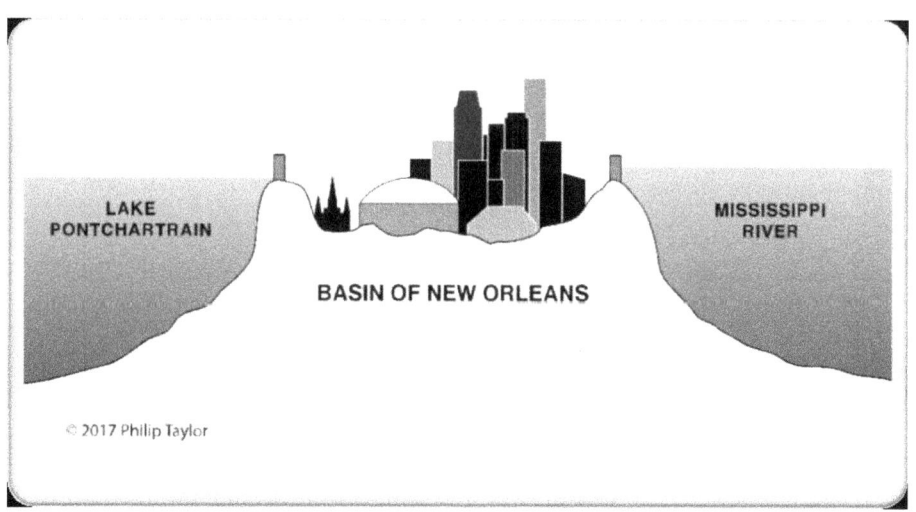

- Since 70 percent of Earth's surface is covered with water, there's potential for considerable evaporation.
- With much more moisture in the atmosphere, the air becomes supersaturated with warm water vapor.
- As that moisture-laden air passes over or through a cooler environment, the water condenses and falls.
- With more water in the air than ever before in recorded history, rains (floods) will be more severe and more frequent.

Have you counted the flooded cities in the last twenty-four months?[1]

Conversely, when Earth's inland surface is uncommonly hot from temperature change, water vapor fails to condense. No condensation = no rain. When there is nothing to trigger the cooling of the moist vapors, devastating drought can result. Crop failure, catastrophic fires, and reduced water for human consumption are virtually inevitable.

One horrific example can be witnessed in eastern Africa. Previously tillable land—the former breadbasket of the region—cannot be plowed because of its packed, hard crust. Even if it were tilled, nothing could grow in these soils because of a long, severe drought. The results are self-evident. Millions of people are now on the brink of starvation. Without water, there is no way that life in the area can survive. In short:

1. There is already insufficient potable water for the population's basic survival needs. Some estimates predict that twenty million people in eastern Africa may die from starvation this year. (Oh! By the way, 80 percent of the

---

[1] In the United States, we think we have a national crisis when a large city floods and a countable number of people die. In India, where people who have been dealing with floods for hundreds of years, they count their dead by the thousands. Cropland, businesses, homes, and *uncountable* numbers of lives—both animal and human—are lost each year. Imagine, this is getting worse.

American population is unaware of that fact. Talking heads on TV would rather discuss the president's latest tweets.)
2. With drought-related crop failures, there is no food for the people and none for their livestock. Dead animal bodies lie scattered outside towns, villages, and cities, leading to disease and stench.
3. Many pastoral nomads use livestock rather than money. For instance, a family's wealth was previously measured and respected by the number of camels it owns. In many such families, however, livestock have died due to water shortages.
4. The inability to properly process human waste and lack of personal sanitation not only causes diseases that result in slow and miserable deaths, but weakens the bodies of those in the region who remain.

1: Cause and Effect

Without question, industrialization and manufacturing have helped build our country. The United States—indeed, the entire western world—would not be where it is today without the billowing plumes of polluted smoke and poisonous fumes from the chimneystacks of the Industrial Revolution. As the country grew, the pollution in the air and the rivers, quietly and subtly at first, soon began to increase exponentially. It grew to the point that the traditional cleaning and purging methods of nature could not keep up.

Even though pollution was beginning to concern many people (especially in the Eastern US industrial cities), it was by then on its own path. It was driven by (1) demands for profit for company stockholders—industrialists like Andrew Carnegie, Henry Ford, J.D. Rockefeller, J.W. Garrett, and George Pullman, (2) the employment needs of millions in the growing population, and (3) the public's demand for the products being produced.

For the most part, only a relative few were being malicious. Most were simply environmentally naïve, inexperienced, and uninformed. The profit-driven industrialists of the 1790s were living in a time of blissful ignorance, unaware of the seeds of destruction they were sowing. Those men and industries built a nation, endowed universities and libraries, changed worldwide civilization, and unknowingly began the process of poisoning their surroundings. They were ignorant of the cause-and-effects relationship of what they were doing, so *they* cannot be blamed.

If they can't, who can?

In no endeavor or field of development were humans ever as environmentally *uninformed* as we were 225 years ago. As our country grew, we accepted, benefited from, and enjoyed that growth in every possible facet of our lives. Even with the knowledge about the environment that we have today, our inaction is supported by our fear that **any corrective act will interrupt our comfortable ways of life.**

Even though we now understand everything about climate change, we have learned that more than 50 percent of the carbon dioxide driving today's crisis has been released into the atmosphere since 1980. That's amazing. Fifty percent since 1980.

The lack of progress leading to correcting climate change's effects on sea temperature and the fundamental food chain that sustains us, is not because we are still *unaware*…it is that we are selfishly *unwilling*.

Unfortunately, the *they* who did not understand what damage they were doing, has now become *we* who do know what we are doing.

By the 1950s, my high school biology teacher was explaining in detail what was happening in the atmosphere and in the rivers, and warning us of the devastating possibilities. At that time he still called the damage a "possibility." By the 1960s, emerging computer models began to show that greenhouse gases would lead to a warmer climate and started to validate the warnings of the 50s.

People working in university labs and think-tanks, a few politicians, and a growing number of citizens, started to realize what was happening. There was, however, already too much money and too many powerful corporations involved. Far too many jobs were at stake to allow for rational and independent decisions about the lurking danger.

Profit fueled the growth of the very engine that created the problem and that same profit overruled an increasingly self-evident need to stop. With the fear of massive unemployment, immediate profit could not and would not be sacrificed. It was cheaper, easier, and more politically acceptable to disregard the whole thing. Warnings of potential problems were ignored in favor of near-term profit, convenience, and power.

Many years ago, as a student in conversations with one of my state's prominent legislators, I was shocked by his reply, "…but son, that will cost jobs!" Yet no one ever admitted, understood, or questioned the next step. "But sir (I so wanted to say), by doing nothing, in due time, there will be *no* jobs!"

Not so long ago:

- the public didn't know that smoking was bad for your lungs;
- a large southern (and, to some degree, national) economy was built on tobacco profits; and
- movie scenes often had the leading actor with an alcoholic drink in one hand and a cigarette in the other—items portrayed as romantic or sexy, but never as lethal.

When facts on these subjects started to come out from research universities, labs, and hospital intensive care units, they were denied by those making profit from the industry. "Surely, smoking doesn't actually cause lung cancer?"

How did the smokers *and* the cigarette companies rebut the evidence?

- They claimed the facts were false.
- They literally published self-serving lies.
- They spent millions in misleading advertisements.
- They attacked and discredited those delivering the message.

How is any of this different from those who deny climate change?

Our air, our water, and our food are fast becoming lethal…and no one seems to care! You will be told: "That's not so…I do care." Your reply must be, "Oh, that's great! May I enlist you to help?" "We have letters to write, calls to make, presentations to schools and libraries …. How would you like to help?"

Even after decades of ample evidence, educated men, women, and even children continued to smoke cigarettes. My own father, an intelligent engineer with three sons begging him to stop, smoked two packs of unfiltered Camels cigarettes a day. He died with cancer spread throughout his body. In the 1980s, *in the hospital's waiting room* just a dozen feet from his bed, there was an ashtray between every other chair.

Denial of facts like these is not new. It took decades before smoking cessation evolved from being an emotional plea for sanity to an accepted medical reality**.** Even though we're not at 100 percent**,** we've made progress. How did we convert denial to acceptance and action?

Informed persistence!

It is critical to understand that in this smoking scenario, those killed by ignoring these facts were only killing themselves (and sometimes those who lived with them). They were not eliminating the habitat of all life.

One can't say "It's not my problem! I don't smoke." Everyone paid the price. Hundreds of thousands of uninsured hospitalized patients flooded emergency rooms and nursing homes, struggling to breathe and unprepared for overwhelming financial consequences. Every taxpayer eventually paid for the damage as insurance companies were forced to raise health care rates and unpaid hospital cost were absorbed by the non-smokers. There were millions of lost hours of productive employment. Within a short time, Health insurance premiums went up for everyone, and ill patients received subsidized public care as required by law and by humanity.

How does this relate to climate change?
What's the coronation?

It is not fair to say that smokers *ignored* the facts because, in both their hearts and minds, they understood the consequences. The issue was (and still is) that ***they chose immediate gratification over long-term consequences***; they knowingly chose the satisfaction of immediate pleasure over later misery, expense, and hastened death. They were sure that *they* were going to be the individuals who would "miss that bullet"…that nothing bad would happen to them.

The similarity is that human behavior continues, and immediate gratification and denial overshadows even the inevitability of death.

If you take nothing else away from this reading, understand that:

*The horror of their denial is that, unlike cigarettes,
in the case of climate change (previously known as global warming),
those who fail to heed the warning,
who blindly perpetuate this behavior of denying the facts, and
who think that nothing bad will happen,
are not only killing themselves and those immediately around them
(as the smokers did for generations), but
they are killing you, the food chain that supports you,
the environment you live in, and
the natural home of generations yet unborn.*

Facts are not open to interpretation!

- In 1975, high in the Andes, the largest glaciers in South America were still growing each year.
- In 2010, those glaciers were turning into large lakes.
- In 1900, the nearly pristine white gloss of a vast range of glaciers in the Himalayas reflected the sun's heat.
- In 1960, black soot from industrialized Europe and Asia covered the previously reflective shine to create a solar-panel effect on glacial surfaces. This has kicked off a period of melting such that the glaciers are expected to disappear by the end of the twenty-first century.
- In 1910, when Glacier National Park was established in Montana, it had 150 glaciers.
- In 2017, there are only twenty-six dwindling glaciers left in the park—some barely identifiable.

Far too many powerful people in authority today are trying to "talk it away." They are ignoring urgent warning signs. As always, they are disregarding the facts because the public is allowing them to. (Please read that again: "…they are disregarding the facts because the public is allowing them to.") You run a risk of being mocked if you dare to ask fundamental questions. In this case, they are not rhetorical.

Who needs clean water and breathable air?
Who needs dry, habitable, arable land?
Who needs a food chain?

Eventually, slowly at first, but well underway by the 1950's, some scientists and a few citizens were beginning to ask these questions. Yet, even then, the public was, by and large, uninterested and remained quiet.

*****

How would the naysayers respond to a story that started like this?

"Farmer Jones, I'm sorry to bother you, but you must be careful! There's a poisonous snake lurking out of sight in your pile of firewood."

The farmer replies:

"I'm too busy to take care of that right now, but later, when it gets colder, and I need to warm my house, *I'll send my daughter to gather the firewood from that pile where the deadly snake lives."*

We have long known that there is an unseen danger lurking in our environmental "woodpile." Having been made aware of the dangers, some citizens and legislators deny the warning, consciously choosing to send the next generation to fetch the wood…to face the snake.

Unaware at first, past generations pulled the firing pin from the most destructive grenade ever conceived by man, and the countdown to devastation started ticking quietly. Not knowing exactly how to handle this persistent ticking, they chose—much like the two-pack-a-day smoker—to ignore it, pretend it would go away, pretend it's not real, pretend it won't happen to them.

Many people in and out of government eventually came to understand the problem's criticality. They reluctantly admitted that the countdown to disaster had started, and yet they *still* chose the easy way out. They tossed the live grenade on to the next generation. They collectively breathed a sigh of relief since they realized that the explosion won't happen on their watch.

*If the young people of this generation fail to take charge,
and if they fail to act as if their future life depended
on their action,
then the grenade will likely explode in their faces.*

If you think that's too dramatic...if you think that's overly alarmist...

- Just identify the hundreds of extinct animal species over the last fifty years, and imagine yourself asking them how they feel about it.
- Just look around the world, identify the millions of people who do not have clean air to breathe or clean water to drink, and ask them if they're worried.
- Just visit the Glacier National Park in Montana, and ask an aging park ranger, "Where are the glaciers?" and listen to her long lost stories.
- Just ask the inhabitants of the islands around the world where finishing villages once thrived, and ask, "Where is your home, your business, your pier?"

We have evolved into a nation who thinks we can get ourselves out of any jam by introducing "new technology"...that science is the answer to almost everything. This massive challenge, however, cannot be solved by a new app. Ten thousand people die somewhere in the world each day simply from the effects of contaminated air. No fancy, expensive filter in the sky will resolve that. Wind, sun, and currents are free, and yet we pursue *fracking* (injecting chemicals under high pressure deep underground) to extract the last drops of fossil fuel.

If you still find this description too dramatic or alarmist, and if you think you can pass this problem on to yet one more generation, then guess what? *You have run out of time!* Your children will suffer life-threatening repercussions from your inaction. Like old Ca'put's warning, "Will they be the last generation?"

Unfortunately for all of us, *the greatest generation* (young adults during the World War II era about whom we hear so much today) were only *selectively* great. They really did accomplish some amazing, almost impossible things. In the process, however, they left a trail of debris. Truly, that generation had several blind spots.

*I know…I was there…I was one of them, and
I was an ineffective messenger.*

*****

The Voice of the Skeptics

In the process of researching this book, I wanted to learn what climate change skeptics had to say, and I wanted to understand their rationale. Climate change is one of the more politically charged topics of our day. It would be impossible to articulate skeptics' personal motives for such thinking without speculation.

We know that 97.1 percent of the thousands of researchers, scientists, and academics surveyed agree that there's persistent and long-term warming across large swaths of land and ocean, that the situation is predominantly man-made, and that it is a threat growing exponentially.

While most well-read people concur, only about half of the broader public accepts the evidence. The public's lack of knowledge and laissez-faire attitude is largely a result of misinformation. One talk radio host conspiratorially claimed that the US National Weather Service predicts upcoming floods and hurricanes far in advance so as to sell more bottled water and emergency supplies. In other instances, ardent nonbelievers argue it is *all* a hoax.

NOW… people other than environmentalists and subject matter experts are increasingly paying attention. When…

- subway lines in New York City fill with seawater, governmental agency leaders become concerned.
- rising seas are causing coastal cities to raise their roads in hopes of keeping tourist-supported economies from failing, entrepreneurs demand action.

- farmlands are endangered by seawater infiltration, heat and drought, producers and consumers begin to focus.
- the potential for collapse of our civil system is a pending reality and when mass civil disobedience based on instinctive survival mode is a growing risk, law enforcement gets interested.
- US military bases, equipment, and personnel around the world are threatened by extreme weather conditions and civil unrest, the Pentagon prepares.

The human repercussions will be catastrophic.

It seems nearly every week, there's a new scientific report published that finds Earth's long-term warming trend is speeding up more quickly than first expected. In this book we discuss the idea that this phenomena "feeds on itself. As one example of this phenomena, surfaces on polar caps are becoming increasingly darkened from man-made pollution that's traveled far, causing ice to absorb heat from the sun's rays where once it was reflected. Warmed water seeps through cracks in glaciers. The cracks grow larger, weakening huge slabs of ice and enabling even more warmed water to flow to the underbelly of glaciers, melting them from the bottom up at an accelerating rate.

As the public comes to understand and see more devastating manifestations of our changing climate, we must hope that that knowledge and experience translates into action. The higher the knowledge level about and understanding of the subject, the higher the acceptance of the pending crisis.

The question remains:
When will that understanding
generate enough fear
to translate into action?

2: Understanding the Basics

Please allow me one paragraph of pondering:

Observe how easily the following scenario unfolds. While the details are complicated, the concept is unusually simple. With very little effort, everyone / anyone can soon understand the problem. Understanding will hopefully generate involvement. (Readers with a greater interest in complexity of global warming should review the Spidergram at the end of this chapter.) I hope it will make it easier for you to explain to others—especially to the skeptics and the uninformed. Please study it slowly and deliberately (this is not a subject to reduce to skimming.) The better you digest the facts, the better you understand the problem, the better you will be able to explain it to others. Your ability to describe the seriousness of the situation is our first step in solving the problem. Climate change skeptics must be educated with facts as well as concepts … and slowly converted.

The depth of <u>your</u> understanding will lead you to wisdom.
Wisdom is a <u>step above</u> being a subject matter expert.
It is knowing what to do with what you know.
Your wisdom is crucial to the solution because
it will allow you to reveal the urgency of the situation and
point the direction toward a solution…
You will soon come to understand
the horrible consequences
of inaction.

Tolerable Degrees of Variation

All of the adults you know are aware of and will concede that mountain climbers and beachgoers can withstand wide variations of temperature. They do so with little to no threat to their survival. In fact, some people deliberately seek out and enjoy extreme differences in temperature for their everyday pleasure.

The tolerance, and even the preference, for a wide temperature fluctuation is absolutely no problem to those of us in the human species. Some people love the warmth of lying on the beach, where it may get to be one hundred degrees, while some love the chilled wind in their faces from a downhill ski slope, where temperatures can be twenty-five degrees or lower. While these variances are wide, remember they are not only *tolerated*, they are purposefully *sought*.

Following that same logic, some people keep their houses unusually warm in winter, and others keep their homes extremely chilly in the summer. Some actually make the choice to spend more to keep their air-conditioners turned down low in summer than they do to heat their houses in winter. Remember, however, in most cases, humans consciously *select and control* the desired temperature of their environments. Even though different folks apply artificial means to control these temperatures, they will not die if the temperature they prefer is changed significantly. It is easy to see that humans have learned to tolerate and even, in some cases, seek out temperature fluctuations of over one hundred degrees.

Keep in mind that humans can tolerate a wide deviation in the degree fluctuation of their environment and that that difference—*a comparatively wide variation*—is not only extreme, it is rare among living species. For humans, that wide but tolerable deviation in temperature is among the widest of most living creatures.

When the sun is shining brightly and there is no wind, a fifty-five-degree day may seem pleasant. When there is a cool breeze blowing and we are in the shade, an eighty degree day seems equally pleasant. We experience thirty to fifty-degree variations without thinking much about it. When the deviation is wider than that, we can simply slip on or off a sweater or change the thermostat.

With proper protective clothing, humans can even go much lower or much higher than these day-to-day examples. Documented normal tolerances for human existence are even wider than a hundred-degree variance:

- Inuit people living in the Canadian Arctic region survive in environments with nighttime temperatures as low as negative 40 degrees.
- Touareg nomads living in the Sahara Desert survive with daytime temperatures that exceed 120 degrees.

That means that humans have learned to exist within an environmental temperature range of 160 degrees.

With these numbers in mind, it looks like we do not have to worry about global warming—as far as temperature alone is concerned—for human survival; not for a long time. Temperature alone is therefore not thought to be our immediate concern by many, even though our discussions are titled "climate change" and "global warming."

Here's the dilemma. Because human tolerance for extreme temperature fluctuation is so big, *it is difficult to get everyone's attention about a two-degree rise in sea or air temperatures.* Many underinformed people (some, unfortunately are our lawmakers and budget approvers) cannot think beyond their own human experience. Temperature changes of "just two degrees" are perceived by most folks as trivial. For now, let's admit that we humans will be OK for a couple hundred years, as far as temperature increase *alone* in concerned. If that is so, if we are going to be OK for several hundred years, why worry? Why get involved?

Unfortunately, humankind does not sense a pending disaster because it is ignoring the details.

The difference between 32 degrees and 34 degrees Fahrenheit is only two.
It is also the difference between ice and water.

This climate warming process *was* all moving gradually, and it *was* easy to go unnoticed. Procrastination seemed to be a reasonable option. Unfortunately, the speed of change has accelerated exponentially in recent years. At the same time, while many humans are (by mechanical heating and cooling devices) coping successfully with that change, most other species cannot compensate. The inability for certain plants and animals to tolerate even the smallest temperature changes—even as little as a two degrees—is spelling their extinction.

So, what's the big deal?

Spidergram

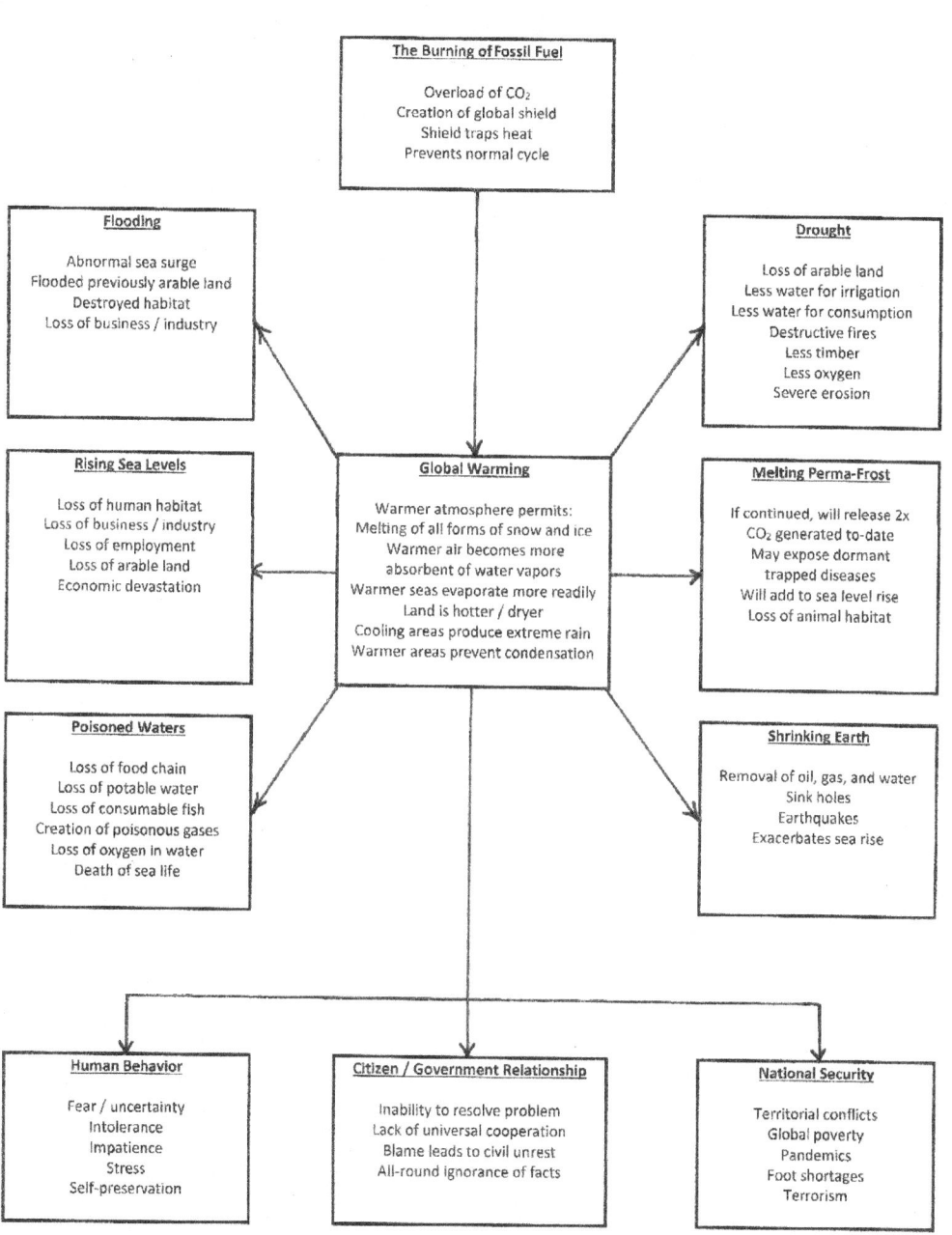

3: Institutionalized Procrastination

Let's begin with two real life examples of people's appetite for denial, one short, and the other a bit longer.

Denial #1: When a guy you know starts to go bald, often the first thing he tries to do is a comb-over. That is, combing his few remaining hairs over the balding spot to attempt to mask what's happening. He remains hopeful that no one will notice. Unfortunately, he is naïve and grossly uninformed to think no one will ever notice. He quietly thinks that it due time, it may reverse itself and go away. This poor fellow refuses to face the reality of his genes and that refusal allows him to live in total denial.

All of us who are bald understand his desire to avoid the inevitable. The reality is that neither a comb-over or a wig nor denial will change the inevitable result.

Denial #2: Your town council knows very well that a metal bridge on the main road into town has deteriorated badly. It hasn't been painted or repaired for decades. They know that the town will experience decline without it, as it is the gateway to Main Street. Engineers declare that the bridge will soon weaken to the point of being dangerous -- even condemned -- perhaps it's already beyond the point of repair. Even though it is the town's main connection to the rest of civilization, council members unanimously say, "It would cost a fortune to scrape, repair, weld, and paint that bridge. We would have to raise the taxes." Politicians have perfected the art of:

- not admitting the *criticality* of the problem,
- not admitting the *urgency* of their action, and
- not having the courage and discipline to explain why the taxes must be raised. (Consider Flint, Michigan.)

If the members of your town council decide (and here is the punchline): "Even if they don't address the problem now, they're confident the bridge won't fall down and kill anyone during *their* term in office." Maybe the *next* elected officials will have the courage to raise taxes needed to repair the bridge.

There will surely be a failure of the bridge at some point. Even a school bus could fall through the rusted bridge. Everyone in the town will then ask, "How did *you* let this happen?" Finger-pointing will start, and you will finally have everyone's attention. At last, the validity of previous voices warning of a looming disaster will be acknowledged. But by then, it will be too late. The penalty of procrastination and avoidance will have come due.

A preventable disaster now becomes an irreversible tragedy.

That's worth repeating: ***Irreversible Tragedy***.

These two real-life examples are not intended to be trivial warnings. They simply reflect existing human behavior at work; the same behavior which is killing the earth's environment. In spite of actions for which we absolutely know the "cause and effect" results, besides realities that are widely understood and accepted, warnings of the results *are continually ignored.* (Smoking, drinking, drugs, infrastructure, etc.) The unfortunate problem is that:

- *When bad behavior becomes so pervasive that it threatens to overpower us, but when we don't see an easy way to change it, it becomes **tolerated.***
- *Perceived as annoying that tolerated behavior slowly establishes itself as **routine**.*
- *Soon thereafter, the routine becomes **accepted** behavior.*
- *The problem with becoming normal, is that once intolerable behavior becomes **ignored**.*
- *As soon as that process is completed, the bad behavior has firmly established itself as a **new norm** and the problem is forgotten.*

What does this have to do with climate change trends or the food chain? It has to do with one's ability to understand that these are the same people who avoid the warnings and deny the causes and inevitable effects unfolding before our eyes.

The deniers:
- must be informed, educated, and convinced that there is a problem;
- must be converted to become financial and political supporters of the clearly defined changes, and
- must understand the need for acceptance of significant lifestyle changes.

Is it too late?
Has global warming become the new (accepted) norm?

The absence of and the corruption of civil discourse, as well as the lost opportunities for advances via traditional cross-pollination of ideas, helps to explain why climate change is not being acted on with the urgency it deserves. If your biology teacher explains that there is a looming crisis and your President tells you it's all a hoax, you may tend to take the easier path, listening to those who reinforce your current beliefs or offer an easier way to avoid involvement and action.

Recall that not so long ago, these are the same people were convinced:

- gay individuals should be "treated" with electroconvulsive shock treatments as mental patients;
- interracial marriages were against God's will and should be illegal;
- black athletes should not be allowed to play on white teams;
- soldiers dying for their country should be separated into platoons by race;
- black workers should have a different pay scale than whites;
- women were not qualified to vote; and never forget…
- witches in Salem should be stoned to death.

These are also the same people and the same mind set and behaviors claiming today that:

- global warming is a hoax;
- the term *climate change* is less offensive—more politically correct;
- more coal mining means more jobs; and especially
- America alone can't make a difference, so why try.

Surely, you have seen that he who has the loudest voice is not always the best informed. The ability to purchase the biggest bullhorn does not equate to having the wisdom to use it. Yet we are cowardly, allowing bullies with the biggest, loudest voices to establish the rules. It is time for this generation to get its own bullhorn and shout vigorously *with an informed and passionate voice.*

You will hear from the politicians, as I did in the 1950s, "It's a cost thing!" or "It's a jobs thing." The predictable consequences of not spending money now are always ignored. Our country's decision in 2017 to withdraw from the Paris Climate Accord was done predominantly in the name of "saving jobs." (That's simply a false premise, spoken with great authority to the uninformed.)

Where is the loud rebuttal saying that without the correction to climate change, rising seas, and clean water, *there will be no jobs?*

Where is the loud rebuttal saying that natural, renewable energy technologies and resources *are* rapidly becoming efficient and cost-effective? *Where are the voices?*

Television's talking heads, acting as news reporters, are rarely informed enough to intelligently rebut climate-change deniers they interview. This leaves the viewing public even more skeptical or doubtful. The shallow thinking, misinformation, and excuse-making that you may hear are attempts to ignore life's "inconvenient truths." Legislators and the voters who put them there all hope that "it won't get too bad." That is, at least, not in the immediate future, "not on my watch." If elected officials pretend it's not too serious and if they refuse to acknowledge it, maybe the problem won't have to be addressed by them during their elected term. Society is allowing self-interested and underinformed legislators to purposely pass the responsibility of mitigating the problem on to the next generation. They fail to understand or even admit that at some nearing point, the situation can no longer be passed on; it will have become irreparable.

In the past, procrastination has *not* often been genuinely catastrophic. It was rarely a fatal error. Not fixing a road or not repairing a bridge or a roof was not devastating; more typically, it was just aggravating. Even that school bus crashing through the old bridge, resulting in the deaths of schoolchildren will be largely forgotten in a few years.

Conversely, the issues we are about to discuss will not—cannot—be forgotten. This problem is no longer a short-term, *tolerable* problem:

- These issues are beyond *inconvenient*.
- The devastation is *verifiable*.
- The results will soon near *catastrophic*.
- The process is rapidly becoming *irreversible*.

Dare I ask you to read those four bullets again?

> Can you sell this to the deniers? *Verifiable… catastrophic… irreversible…*

These issues are accelerating exponentially every hour of every day that we are trapped in inaction. This very nature of the cause-and-effect syndrome ensures that the deterioration will continue at an increasing rate. For example:

- Once an ocean kelp farm has died, the foundation of the sea's food chain is gone. Not damaged… gone!
- Without kelp acting as the womb of the sea's food chain, all else will fail.
- A coastal city cannot be inhabited when it's under salt water and the tide never recedes.
- A species can become extinct only once.
- Seals and polar bears are dying from starvation and exhaustion, and we know why.

Allow me to deviate from the theme for two short and regrettably true stories about careless extinction:

1) In 1970, I moved to Maryland's Eastern Shore. For the first time in my life, I came in contact with the annual arrival of

thousands of tiny black frogs. They did no damage and only stayed a few weeks. These creatures were so small and charming that a single adult could easily sit on my thumbnail. I didn't know what significance they had in the cycle of life, but I do know that they were a part of the wonder of living in a rural setting. With the introduction of herbicides and pesticides, farm fields like mine became more like a picture in an agricultural textbook; no weeds, no pests, and plants standing tall and healthy. One year, however, I noticed that there were just a few hundred frogs in the spring, and the following year, only a few dozen. The following year, there were none. No one ever mentioned their absence.

2) My Eastern Shore farm came with a reciprocal agreement between the new owner and an Amish man from Delaware. The Amish man kept five beehives on the edge of a large field and occasionally harvested the honey. Not only did we have the offer of free honey, but our crops and trees flourished because of pollination by tens of thousands of bees. One four-foot tall American Holly tree had so many berries, it glowed like a red mass in the morning sun. Within just five years of the introduction of chemical agents to improve the crops, however, the bee population was gone. Tens of thousands of tiny corpses lay around the hives. No reproduction, no honey, no pollination, and an anemic Holly.

In short, within my first five years on the farm, by innocently leveraging guidance of Maryland state agricultural department resources, I had unwittingly facilitated the elimination of two local species in a 152-acre area.

Human interference with the balance of nature
can be devastating...
Believe it!

*****

Previous generations of adults have had their chance, and some have demonstrated that they care little about your hometown's old bridge or, for that matter, your children's welfare or anything beyond *their* narrow, immediate comfort and interests.

As long as these issues *can be ignored*, in other words, and as long as the old bridge is still standing, there will be no action. As long as there is air to breathe in Washington, DC, and dry ground on which to build another monument, there will be inaction. (Politicians passing through the nation's capital are often unaware that well-known portions of the city are at sea level and built on filled wetlands; within sixty years some will be submerged by rising water.) In their mind, until they are inundated with intense pressure *from the same voters who sent them there*, they will continue to assume it is politically acceptable and economically prudent to do nothing.

*I have had decades of local, state, and national governmental experience,
and I guarantee you that elected officials
will respond to articulate constituent pressure!*

*Again…as long as the bridge hasn't fallen,
there will be no action.
When it finally falls from the weight of a loaded
elementary school bus,
it will be too late…*

and it will be irreversible.

4: How Bad Can It Really Be?

How bad is it? Doubters should have the opportunity to ask the residents of Beijing, "Why are you wearing a face mask?" especially on a day when they cannot see the color of a traffic light from their car or bike. Ask people choking on polluted air in Iran, India, or Cameroon:

- Where did your clean, breathable air go?
- How long can you survive this way?
- What are you and your government doing about it?

You may not be popular for bringing up these points, for discussing them, or even for letting anyone know that you are thinking about them. Their very mention can trigger a firestorm of debate by skeptics. Some people will tell you that you need not worry about the future of civilization. Some of the people whom you respect, even some in positions of authority, will chastise you. You may hear concerns described as alarmist, disrespectful, arrogant, and overly dramatic. I know this to be true because when I was in high school many years ago, my state legislators called me these things. However, never was I called *uninformed*.

Nevertheless, discuss it you must. Never let anyone call you uninformed! Familiarity with accumulated data assures an informed and effective conversation.

After the discussion comes action. Your understanding, your enthusiasm, even your ideas for remediation are *nothing* without action. Always remember that any idea without action is just another passing fluffy cloud, beautiful only at the moment it is observed.

Be prepared to be told:

- You do not understand the costs of stemming global warming.
- You do not understand the costs of eliminating water pollution.
- You will understand better when you are older.
- There is no real problem. This is a normal cyclical weather pattern.
- This will all pass in due time. It is nature at work.

People who are committed to this idea will be surprised if you respond:

"Yes! You are correct."

You can acknowledge that there have been several massive weather fluctuations over the eons of Earth's existence. Ice ages and asteroids have eliminated life and reshaped landmasses. You can also acknowledge that humans are fundamentally powerless against those dominant forces of nature. There has been, and will always be, a natural cycle of uncontrollable climate change.

However, the pattern we're experiencing today is not a part of that natural cycle. None of those past events were caused by human interference. None! For the past 250 years, Earth's inhabitants have artificially influenced the balance of nature and thereby are encouraging the early onset of nature's reaction. The speed of the natural process in being exponentially encouraged by pollution—plain and simple.

*Since we now know what that interference is,
all we have to do is stop doing it.*

A quick review:

- If we don't act more purposefully, by the time the adults currently in charge realize and acknowledge that this new generation *does* understand, it may be too late.
- Billions of dollars are being spent ineffectually right now. Money is being wasted on extravagant hydraulically-operated sea walls, huge dykes, unimaginable pumps, and raised roadways in China, Japan, Italy, Korea—even in New York and Florida. Don't forget those government engineer-designed levees in Louisiana. (Please take a minute to look it up.) Refer back to the chart on New Orleans. That city sits in a large valley below sea level. What are our chances for sustained containment of encroaching sea rise?
- We are approaching the point where the situation will be irreversible. There will be millions and millions of people made homeless, the loss of property will be beyond that caused by any natural weather event ever witnessed, and there will be a devastated economy, a shortage of food and drinkable water, and great potential for mass civil disobedience unparalleled in human history. *National* security will not be the problem. Your local neighborhood could be your own private war zone. Hurricane Katrina of 2005 will seem like child's play. It was not even a rehearsal for what you will face.
- If other industrialized nations do act vigorously and feel that they are contributing to real improvement, the United States' inaction will weaken our leadership position on the world stage. National security will be increasingly at risk as we become vulnerable.
- If we reach a point at which *self-preservation mode* kicks in, rules, regulations and norms of conduct guiding human behavior will become irrelevant—a horrible thing to contemplate. (Think of the Donner-Reed wagon party trying to cross Utah's Salt Flats in the 1840s or the Uruguayan rugby team whose airplane wrecked in the Andes in the 1970s. Multiply that times millions!) Rich and poor alike

will be reduced to dreadful survival behavior. Race, age, sex, class, religion, education, nationality, morality, or wealth will matter less than ever before. No one will be able to buy their way out.

The instinct to survive (the first law of nature) will become the only rule...
even though surviving for another day may only be an invitation
to an unbearable experience.

One of the most frustrating parts of this horror story is that, to the uninformed, it will sneak up on us. Many are going to wonder how it happened. Those of us who understand the problem and see it coming will understand that we are in a situation where it's too late to recover.

Balance Ignored

If you put a one-pound bag of sugar on one side of an old-fashioned balance scale and one toothpick on the other side, the world would laugh at your naïveté. If you add one toothpick every day, no one would notice your efforts. However, some day, long after you started the experiment, a day when everyone had forgotten about what day you began, only *one* toothpick will tip the scale. One! The tiny weight of that one final toothpick will allow you to stand, stare, and watch one pound of sugar be overpowered by one toothpick, and the scale will slowly start to rise. The one tiny toothpick will have tipped the balance and overwhelmed the weight of the bag.

Predictably, climate change doubters will say, "All you have to do to correct the situation is remove several toothpicks, and the balance will return."

The problem is that each ecological toothpick is so interrelated to the complicated environment that each is irreversibly bound to the others, and it has become a tiny, inseparable part of the mass. When

the last toothpick falls in place or when the last drop of acidic rain pollutes the ocean to a point of supersaturation, aquatic life will die, and there will be no going back. It will be too late to begin a discussion, form a committee, start an investigation, or find common cause. It will be too late for anyone to get involved.

As we have discussed, the urgency for attention to climate change is often overshadowed by shallow discussions about fanciful trips to distant planets or the possibility of growing tomatoes on the moon. Remember that living in a colony on another planet can only succeed when it is supported by a base station here on Earth. Even if temporary food and shelter are accounted for, health care, entertainment, socialization, selection of a mate, reproduction, and education cannot be duplicated in a spaceship trying to escape the disaster left on this planet. (By the way, a spaceship supplied with what? Even rice can't be grown in paddy fields contaminated with salt water.)

It is vital that you, the next generation, in your upcoming positions in government, politics, and education, even as voting citizens, understand that those billions now being borrowed and spent must be redirected toward dramatically reducing fossil fuel consumption and stemming global warming.

Parents, teachers, and students must take related classroom studies seriously. They must turn accumulated data and information into *wisdom*, which will be the lifeline to success in solving this dilemma. Young students must carefully select their high school and college courses and always work toward learning ways to stop this recklessness. All must understand that without this next generation's immediate involvement, there will be no second chance. In short:

- Prepare yourself to run for public office at every level of government.
- Carefully observe the complicated yet delicate interrelationships and interdependence of everything around you.
- Thoughtfully listen to everything that is being reported by both climate change proponents and deniers.
- Engage in meaningful discussions. Be prepared to offer an intelligent rebuttal.
- Demand facts over opinions, answers over clichés, reason over emotion.
- Be mindful for whom you vote.

At the very least, become a vocal advocate to organize your neighbors, and give them the tools with which to regularly lobby their local, state, and national representatives. We can no longer wish this away. If you're going to spend time on social media, if every thought you type starts with a hashtag, please continue your networking. Just remember, *this* topic needs to become one of your main subjects. With few exceptions, politicians have their heads in the sand, and all they are discussing is how beautiful their tail feathers are.

*****

Earlier, we asked, what's the big deal? Unfortunately, there isn't just one challenge; there are several that are delicately intertwined. They are all coming at us at the same time, and they are feeding on one another. This interrelationship is making the challenges' advance rapid, increasingly strong, and a complicated story to tell.

5: Big Deal #1 - The Food Chain

Even though we previously established that:

1. humans can easily survive a one-hundred and sixty degree variation in the temperature of their environment;
2. larger animals like hogs, sheep, and beef cattle can withstand slightly lesser, but still wide, extremes; and
3. many larger fish and edible sea creatures can also tolerate similar temperature deviations,

…not all of nature's creatures can!

That's *the* critical point: not all animals and plants can tolerate wide temperature fluctuations. Many cannot tolerate more than a comparatively few degrees of fluctuation without dying. Each of those sensitive life forms, which will be killed off by comparatively small changes in temperature, has a role somewhere in the food chain. Each is the intended *dinner* for some other, higher-level species.

Keep the word *tolerance* in mind, not just the word *temperature*. Do not dwell on the actual number. Think about how much a given temperature deviates from the normal temperature that a species can tolerate. Explore the long-standing natural food chain, which we know has sustained life since before recorded history. Let us follow that chain; rather than from the bottom up, we'll turn it upside down and discuss it from the top down in a simplified manner.

Level 1
Since predators no longer routinely eat people, we are fortunate to find ourselves at the top of the food chain. Let's call humans Level 1. We humans, however, *are* the predators to almost everything else. (Remember, we are the ones who can easily tolerate the extreme temperature fluctuations with no harm.)

Level 2
The largest of fish—most of which also tolerate a fairly wide fluctuation in degrees—can also tolerate these variances *without* interference to their lives. Let's call them Level 2. As prime targets for human consumption, many of these have already been "fished out."

Level 3
Midsize and smaller fish, at Level 3, were previously considered less desirable for human consumption, yet they were the very food that sustained larger Level 2 fish. With reduced presence of larger fish, however, smaller fish became more plentiful and gained the notice of the fishing industry. Level 3 fish, now at less risk of being eaten by Level 2 fish, could reproduce and raise their young safely. They could multiply without interference, and these once undesirable fish became plentiful.

With relatively few large fish available for the market, well-equipped and experienced fleets of fishing boats started hauling in tons of these Level 3 fish. The next link of the food chain, previously kept in check by being the food of the larger fish, became the only thing readily available and therefore *marketable*. The Level 1 human consumer demanded *something*, so with the preferred Level 2 fish harder to find and therefore expensive, fishermen gave the market what was available. Commercial fishing operations became efficient predators to the Level 3 medium fish, replacing their natural Level 2 predators.

Level 4

Those midsize and tiny fish in Level 3 feed exclusively on even tinier fish as well as plants and animals that we'll call Level 4. These tiny lives have always fed on seaweed, plankton, and single-cell life forms. They continue to have a reasonably healthy diet at the lower-level food chain. Of course, the same cycle of supply and demand can happen again, only at the lower levels. If we continue to fish out the medium fish, we will be reduced to harvesting and eating the only things left available. There isn't much stuff below Level 4. At this point, we would revert to consuming whatever seaweed might still be alive.

Level 5

The Great Barrier Reef, an enormous series of coral reefs and islands off the northeast coast of Australia, is in danger of dying. All one has to do is wait and do nothing, and those coral reefs will all die. Tiny, soft-bodied polyps (pinhead-size organisms), who build their hard calcium shells into impenetrable mounds of beauty and also are food for many species of tiny fish, are not dying from pollution. They are dying because they can't tolerate the warming waters of the surrounding Coral Sea.

It doesn't take much imagination to predict what will happen when the Level 4 fish have nothing more below them to feed on. If tiny fish don't die from starvation, humans will catch them to the point of extinction. The sea will be empty of life. We cannot survive by consuming single-cell slime.

Note: There are far more than five levels to the sea's complicated food chain. I have greatly simplified the process to make a fundamental, visual representation.

The Sea's Food Chain
(greatly simplified)

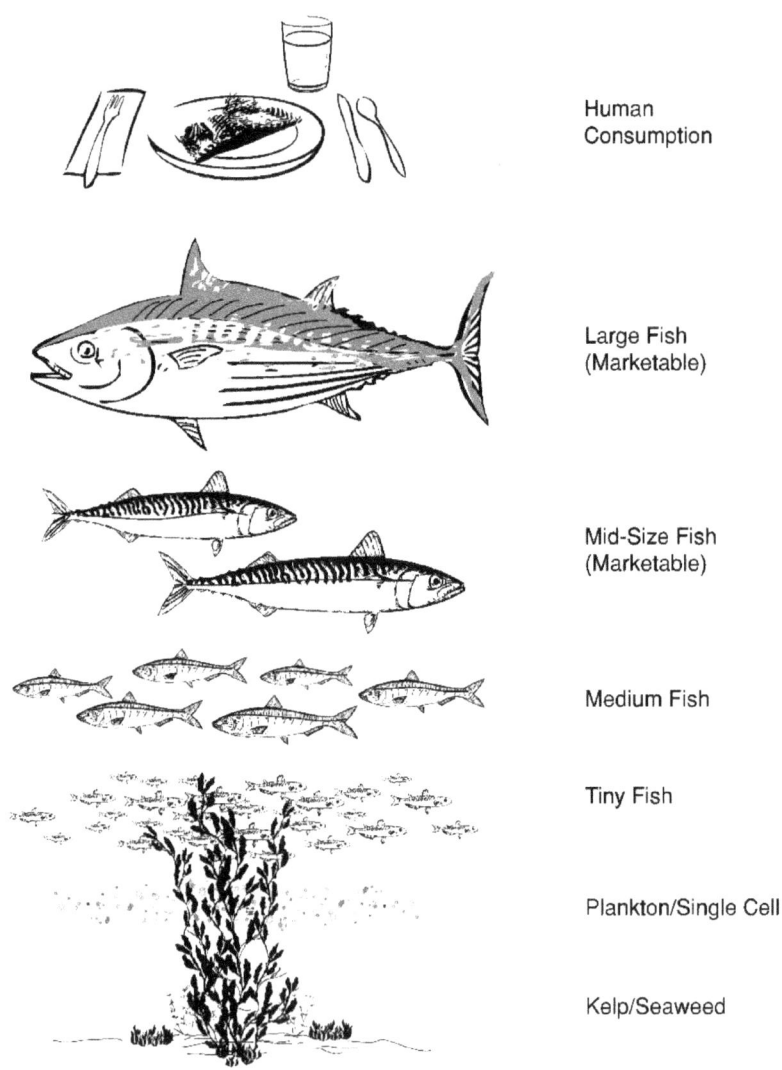

Now, turn your thinking upside down. Ignore for the moment, human intervention by commercial fishing fleets. Let's work our way back up the food chain:

- Level 5 microscopic life at the bottom of every lake and sea, both plant and animal forms, were food for the smallest fish. They all die because they can tolerate only a few degrees of temperature change.
- Level 4 tiny fish now starve because they have nothing to eat. When they were alive, healthy, and plentiful, they become food for the medium fish. But they are now unhealthy and dying.
- Level 3 medium fish are now without a food source. They first weaken, fail to reproduce, and eventually die.
- Level 2 fish, the larger, healthier fish most desirable for human consumption, once fed by the abundance of the now depressed Level 3 fish, are gone.
- Level 1 humans, faced with depletion of consumable sea life, will have lost a primary source of protein. Thousands of villages will lose their main source of employment—fishing—and their main source of protein—fish.

This *was* the balanced food cycle nature gave us. Technology outpaced the natural reproduction of the species and knocked normal environments out of balance.

Unfortunate Observation

Humans (our Level 1 consumers) have always migrated toward and lived near water. There, they caught fish as a large part of their diet and economy. In addition to food, water provided transportation and recreation. As humans became more experienced and their fishing techniques improved, they gained the ability to more rapidly and efficiently catch bigger fish, those highest on the aquatic food chain.

The looming consequences of those advancements were barely noticed at first. For several thousand years, the healthy reproduction of these bigger fish (our Level 2 link) was able to keep up with the demand of the fishermen's market as it supplied the population's demands. In the last 150 years, however, with the introduction of power boats and gigantic fishing nets combined with increasing market demand by Level 1 human consumption of Level 2 products, fishermen have been able to catch so many of the larger species that, in many cases, adult breeding stock cannot keep up with replenishing the supply. Humans have scraped off so many of the Level 2 creatures at the top layer of the sea's food chain that several species have recently been removed from the sea to the point of extinction. Once large and plentiful Level 2 creatures on the food chain have dwindled dangerously low.

Once, while on a trip to New England, I saw a large lobster mounted on the wall of a fishing-pier seafood restaurant. It was reported to have weighed over forty pounds when it was caught in the early 1900s. Yet today, that same menu was advertising "one-pound lobster tails." What once passed as large-size fish not very long ago is now gone.

Irony

Many fish that survive into adulthood but are caught later in their life have become so toxic from polluted waters that they are now deemed uneatable. To complicate the large fish dilemma, chemical pollution and particulates emitted into the air (the very process that leads to our main topic of climate change/global warming) are pulled down by rain and deposited in ever-increasing amounts in lakes, streams, rivers, and seas.

In addition to chemical pollutants, plastics and other man-made contaminants are accumulating by the acre—some floating in mammoth island-like reefs, some sinking to the bottom suffocating coral, bottom feeders, and seaweed. That which *does* eventually dissolve, poisons the water so that the fish are unhealthy or uneatable to humans and to each other.

Seafood, *at all levels* of the food cycle, eat, take in, and absorb those chemicals in volumes *that they cannot process*. Unable to pass all of the undesirable intake out through their waste, their flesh and muscles absorb the poison ... the chemicals ... the pollutants. The fish, no longer healthy, do not reproduce as they had for thousands of years *and* they are no longer a good food source for humans or natural predators.

Larger predators, unaware of any danger, continue to consume whatever is available at the level below them, and they too become saturated with the same contaminants. Now, both their water *and* their food are contaminated. If they *do* somehow manage to mature in their contaminated waters, and we dare to eat those fish from any level, we humans, in turn, are contaminated.

I recently read a 2018 food label warning that halibut, sea bass, bluefish, some tuna, and some lobsters contain so much mercury that such food should only be consumed occasionally and never eaten by pregnant women or unhealthy people.

Nice Try

In a misbegotten attempt to circumvent pollution and contamination, aquaculture farmers are actually catching baby tuna *by the ton* and resettling them into domestic fattening tanks. However, they are finding that fish raised in the artificial environment of fattening tanks and aquaculture ponds are, in many ways, far more costly than wild-caught blue fin tuna. Such tuna can only be fed one of two things:

1. Fifteen pounds of otherwise marketable Level 3 fish per pound of sushi harvested. or
2. A diet of Level 3 fish caught and ground into domestic fish food pellets.

Unfortunately, tuna don't recognize pellets made from ground-up fish as desirable as live food, so farmers attempt to "teach" the fish to eat the pellets. The tuna must gobble them quickly before they sink to the bottom among the fish droppings, where they become inedible. *The waste is exponential.*

Since the survival rate among these wild-caught but farm-raised baby tuna is not high, farmers are now trying to breed and raise tuna to replace the ones caught in the wild. That too is not going very well, it is expensive, time-consuming, and has a dubious future.

Lastly, consider the concept of efficiency. Feed Conversion Ratio is a measurement of inputs to outputs used by farmers to describe how efficient an animal is at using its feed. In simple terms, it is the rate at which one food is converted into another higher-level food. Some examples of this:

- to produce one pound of chicken, about two pounds of feed is required
- to produce one pound of pork, about four pounds of feed is required
- to produce one pound of beef, more than six pounds of feed is required

While beef is the least efficient of these animals in using its food, in *all* these cases note that grain-based food can currently be replenished each year.

Compare that to sushi as mentioned above. It takes a whopping *fifteen* pounds of small fish to grow one pound of sushi. In other words, humans could have eaten fifteen pounds of smaller fish for every pound of domestic sushi they consumed. Remember, these

Level 3 fish are under tremendous strain of depletion due to an unbalanced food chain and contaminated habitat.

*****

That's Only One Part of the Problem

Earlier, we discussed the ability of some living creatures to tolerate wide ranges of temperature change. We know that humans can stand extreme changes and that whales have migrated annually from the frigid arctic seas to tropical waters for thousands of years. However, we have not yet explained and established that *there are unquestionable limits of toleration for almost all species, and that tolerance varies widely.* As a rule (there are a few odd exceptions), the span of that temperature deviation is rarely the hundred degrees the human species can tolerate—but the variation is *less tolerable* in smaller species. Five or ten degrees to a beaver are not the same as five or ten degrees to a much smaller rodent.

We also know of those rare exceptions where organisms live in subzero ice packs and superheated volcanic ash. They are, in every sense of the word, microscopic exceptions and a purely biological anomaly.

Elephants

Let's use an elephant as an example of a very large species and discuss its tolerance for temperature change and why "temperature" when taken alone, is rarely a singular problem. We know that both Asian and African elephants have been transported from their warm native climates to zoos all over the world. Some must face occasionally cool temperatures and, in some areas, even long winters with snow.

We still can't figure where he got them from, but Hannibal is reported to have used elephants to cross the Alps on his way to attack Rome in 218 BC. Somehow, they tolerated that frigid journey. We do know that the ancestors of today's elephants had a much thicker layer of fat, with long, shaggy fur, allowing them to go into some very cold areas. Today's elephants—African, Indian, Chinese—prefer warm climates.

Paradoxically, hot temperatures are more dangerous to elephants than cold conditions. Today's elephants, when living in their natural habitats, need huge volumes of water and fresh greens. As global warming leads to less drinkable water and reduced vegetation for free-range elephants, the ability of these animals to survive is being markedly reduced. Their poor diet directly disrupts their reproductive cycles, and the likelihood of giving live, healthy births diminishes.

There are pockets of elephant populations where herds are being squeezed into smaller and smaller ranges due to overpopulation by humans and land-clearing for agriculture. These animals become hungry, overcrowded, and stressed. In many cases they rebel, destroy villages, and kill people. Reports about "rogue" elephants are leading to demands for herds to be thinned due to overpopulation.

This loss of their natural habitat is also reducing the healthy gene pool due to inbreeding. This, in turn, is further creating unhealthy offspring, who will have a difficult time obtaining the food and water necessary for *their* healthy growth and reproductive cycles. An unhealthy adult elephant will have less interest in breeding, and hungry bulls will rant and rage to the point of destruction.

Whether it is a hot day or a cold night, an extreme fluctuation of many degrees will not *directly* kill an elephant. The resulting droughts brought on by extreme weather changes, the loss of water and vegetation driven by these weather changes, and crowding *will*. Therefore, we quickly see that *warming* alone is not the problem. The disruption that persistent warming causes to the balance of nature leads to the loss of green habitat and the absence of water for drinking, bathing, and cooling. Over time, extreme temperature variations will—indirectly—drive elephants and other large land mammals toward extinction.

Pika

In the Grand Teton Mountains in Wyoming, there lives a cute little creature called a Pika. It is a cousin to the rabbit and, like its cousin, lives on grasses and green leaves. The pika is a chubby rodent that scurries among the rocks, trying to avoid (in yet another food chain) becoming a meal for bald eagles and other predatory birds. From the grand elephant to this tiny pika, Earth's warming and changing climate is threatening their environments in similar ways. Please notice this parallel scenario.

The rocks among which the pika scurry and the air they breathe at the lower levels of the mountains *are being heated* well above their normal, traditional temperature ranges. Since pika *cannot survive* at a temperature much above seventy-five degrees, each year they have migrated farther up mountains, searching for cooler environments. While animals normally migrate when searching for food and water, pika are being forced to move to higher elevations in search of a cooler climate.

One could smile and think, "Ah, nature at work. The pika is solving its own global warming problem." The devastating but less obvious situation is this: up where the air and the rocks are cooler (seventy-five degrees or lower), the area is more open, rockier, and grows less vegetation. The pika, now forced into an area that provides a poor diet, must spend more time in the open searching for food.

With less vegetation for cover, the openness makes pika easy targets for predators—both four-footed and winged. (Do you notice the parallel pattern here? The seeds for the extinction of the pika have already been sown.) When you consider restricted environment, inferior diet, disrupted reproduction cycle, and increased vulnerability to predators, it is not difficult to anticipate the results.

A point we have discussed several times and a point I urge you never to forget:

Global warming is not a single, isolated, easy-to-solve problem.
It touches every other facet of every living thing on this planet.
All life, plant and animal, has evolved in and learned to tolerate
certain temperature ranges: certain highs and lows
beyond which they cannot survive.
We are irreparably changing that firmly established environment,
the very one in which all creatures evolved and have
thus far survived.
That very act of survival is in danger.

*****

Indirect Consequence

According to an article by Christopher Solomon in the June 2017 issue of *National Geographic*, we learn that after ten thousand years of successful reproduction, sea tortoises may be facing their demise due to warming sand. Solomon reports that the warm sand influences the sex of the forming fetus and that the warmer the sand, the more tortoise females there are.

Follow that logic to its inevitable conclusion (and as reinforcement of the previous statement):

**We are irreparably changing their firmly established environment,
the very environment in which all creatures evolved
and have thus far survived.
We are altering nature's balance!**

With fewer and fewer males, the repopulation of this ancient creature is doomed. Mr. Solomon goes on to describe the similar fate of the iguana. The warming temperatures of the Pacific Ocean around the Galápagos Islands, six hundred miles off the coast of Ecuador, are killing previously plentiful algae. The increasing absence of algae is starving iguana, which depend on it for survival. (Make time to read his informative piece one day.)

Once again, it's the *tolerance* for temperature variation in a given animal that matters most in its long-term survival, not the absolute temperature.

*****

Moving Down the Food Chain: Single-Cell Life

Let's consider the smallest among us: an amoeba, algae, a bacterium, a fungus, or any single-cell life creature. Most scientists agree that these organisms were among the first forms of life on Earth. They have lived undisturbed by humans or weather for billions of years.

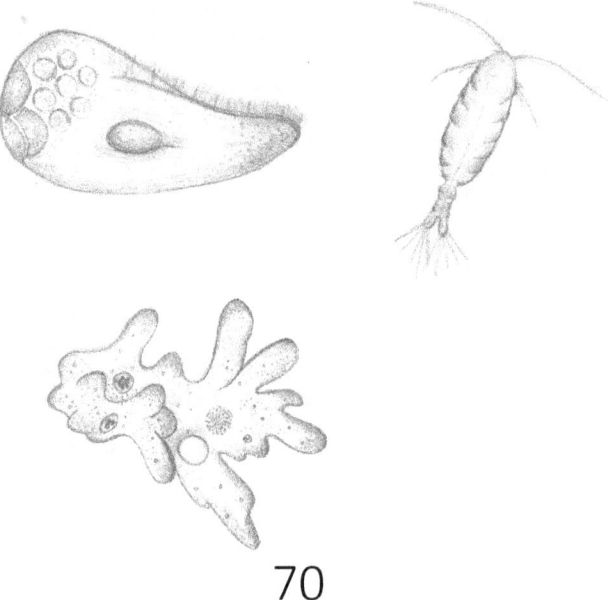

*They live on both land and in the sea,
and they are the very precious beginning of the food chain.*

The tiniest of all sea creatures eat these single-cell life forms, and they (as you will recall) grow to become dinner for the next level up the chain. On and on it goes. Humans have, for many thousands of years, been at the top. Most people are unaware of the criticality of the food chain and don't even think about where it begins. If one does *not* understand its importance, why would he or she promote actions to protect it?

*Here you must become a subject matter expert.
As I have mentioned time and time again,
knowledge will be your ammunition in this battle.
As a subject matter expert, you will be equipped to deal in facts
and
not in suppositions, opinions, or emotions.*

We understand that, if taken one at a time, very few of these tiny individuals *can* tolerate unbelievable *temperatures*, *pressures*, and *acidity* -more than any elephant or human. In the deepest depths of the sea, where pressures are intolerable to human or fish, they survive. In frigid arctic areas and the edges of volcanos, where science once thought nothing could live, we find single-cell creatures surviving. We are not discussing these uncommon, weird exceptions. Don't allow yourself to be dissuaded by these rarities used by critics as examples.

Why, then, is the world discussing *temperature* as if it were *the* problem? Be careful! Always remember that we are not discussing temperature in an absolute sense—we are speaking of temperature *changes,* temperature *tolerances,* temperature *variation.* We are discussing the unique individual tolerance of those changes and distances between what is normal to a specific creatures and what we are doing to change that normal temperature range.

*Earth and all of its creatures have limits on temperature variation,
that is, the range in which they can survive.
When those limits are breached, whether caused by
humans or nature,
and these life forms are unable to tolerate or
adjust to the difference,
they will all die.*

*These ranges of temperature tolerances were a part of
their creation
and are critical to the environment in which they have evolved
and in which they once flourished.*

*Now, both Earth and its inhabitants are being assaulted
by challenges to those limits.
Human behavior is artificially imposing temperature changes
on the environment,
changes that many creatures cannot tolerate.*

*This devastating intrusion on the balance of nature
is unquestionable being brought on by man-made global warming.*

*Global warming is inevitable when one materially alters the
umbrella that covers us
and artificially warms the air trapped under that shield.*

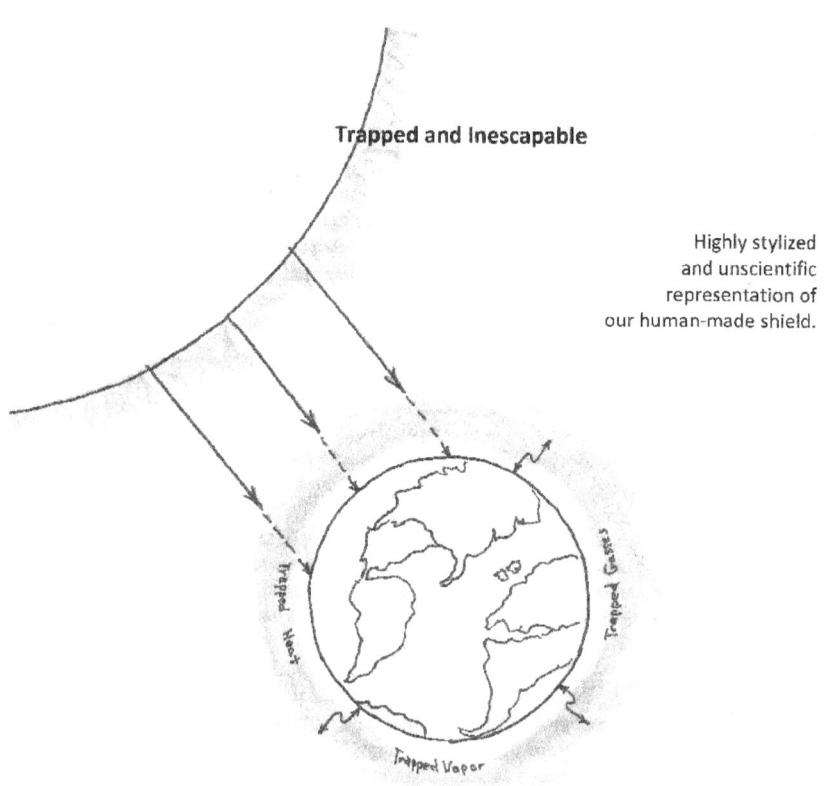

Trapped and Inescapable

Highly stylized and unscientific representation of our human-made shield.

In 250 years, we have succeeded in changing the normal flow and balance of:
    what gets out...
      what gets in...
        what we trap...
          how it circulates.

In 2016, there were far more news reports about infants dying after having been mistakenly left in hot vehicles by careless parents than ever before. Why? In part, young parents may not realize that infants' tolerance to heat variations is *much* narrower than those of a thirty-year-old person like them. A healthy adult can, with difficulty, withstand two or more hours in a closed, sunbaked car with an interior temperature of 120 degrees Fahrenheit, but an infant is likely to face heat stroke within just one hour.

Describing the problem is not as simple as telling teenagers that global warming is bad. It is unfortunate that such innocuous words got into common vernacular. We must start explaining the *inability* of nature itself, and all of its living creatures, to tolerate and survive *the deviation of,* and *the tolerance for*, that temperature *variation.* That very *fluctuation* that humans have created is being forced on, and is irreparably changing, the balance of Earth's ecosystem. Leaders must stop talking about the *number* of degrees in absolute terms. They must be aware of the tolerance for the *amount* of change. With a sustained sea temperature increase of just five degrees, some coral, some plants, and probably the little pika are forever doomed.

Kelp and its criticality

Kelp is the largest of all marine algae. It is not a true plant because it does not obtain its sustenance from roots. It has long been called seaweed because of its long, tough stem, and flowing, plantlike "leaves." It grows abundantly in cool waters wherever the sun can penetrate. Clear, cool water is essential because kelp gets its life support by photosynthesis. The sun must be able to penetrate the depth and clarity of the water. Cloudy, polluted water limits photosynthesis.

Kelp attaches itself to the sea floor by a root-like structure called *holdfast,* which does not provide sustenance to the algae as conventional roots do for plants. Uniquely, at the base of each kelp leaf grows a gas-filled bubble, an air pocket that allows the algae to grow upright and float when detached and to relocate when the algae breaks away.

Huge clusters of kelp are called *forests* and can encompass acres and acres, even miles of sea in one underwater cluster. Kelp forests quickly become the homes for uncountable varieties of the world's tiniest creatures of every description.

Kelp forests are, in every way, the mother of the ocean. Unfortunately, kelp can be killed rather easily. The warmed waters of a recent tsunami damaged vast kelp forests, which have died out completely. Even several degrees above whatever has become their *normal* temperature range and the range of the single-cell creatures that live within its boughs (creatures that are the very foundation of the sea's entire food chain), both lose their natural environment, and they both die. Some will say, "We don't eat single-cell creatures—and most of us don't eat kelp, so why worry?" We must worry because they are the catalyst that starts the very food chain we previously discussed. We must worry because they are the foundation, the base, the womb from which all else in the sea depends.

Unprecedented Urgency

So, when you consider *one* of the devastating results of climate change over time, don't think only about a warmer summer or a colder winter. Don't think only about how you react to a swing of fifty degrees. Remember the tolerance that *other* species have, and consider that *their* ability to accept a sustained variation from normal temperatures before they become extinct may be measured in single-digits. To recap:

- It is *important* to recognize that the number of degrees is not the only factor for limited temperature tolerance.
- It is *critical* to recognize that some species are keenly sensitive to very small temperature fluctuations.

If one or two degrees warmer kills some single-cell life
and if five or six degrees warmer can kill an entire kelp field,
at the present rate of warming,
how much time do you think you have
before the very foundation of the sea's food chain is lost forever?

6: Big Deal #2 - Water

Warming Water

A recent NASA report states that 2016 showed the hottest temperatures ever measured since records began to be kept in 1880. If you look at each of the last ten years sequentially, each year (with one exception) has been hotter than the one before. Both land masses and sea surfaces are absorbing these extraordinary temperatures exactly as a solar panel does on your neighbor's roof.

Warming water in the Gulf of Maine has caused several species previously common in the area to abandon their habitats, according to a February 2017 *National Geographic* article by Cynthia Barnett. The results of this are further examples of the disruption to food chain issues we have discussed. In the article, Barnett reports that puffin chicks are starving because of a shortage of the parents' normally available food of prey.

Farther south, warming water off South Florida has produce algae blooms so bad that beaches had to be closed and tourism has lessened. Hotels and restaurants have lost business, and lifeguards and other workers have lost their livelihoods. How many years of reduced tourist income can that industry manage before declaring defeat? Warming waters have only started to wreak havoc and devastation. Here again, nothing will be done by those with the power to take action until these patterns are consistent—even continual—and then is will most likely be too late.

Water expands when it is warmed. As much as one-third of the ongoing rise in sea levels is caused by thermal expansion. The dirtier the water, be it from natural or man-made forms of pollution, the easier it absorbs heat and the hotter it gets. Warmed waters mixing with chilled waters from melting polar ice are causing changes to longstanding (actually ancient) oceanic currents—to the point that regional sea level changes and travel patterns will begin to vary considerably.

Looking even more broadly:
- While we have known about Earth's long-term warming trend and its potential effects for over fifty years, politicians and citizens alike have chosen to ignore scientists and academics, despite mounting evidence.
- We have known that in addition to natural sources, human activities, such as the burning of fossil fuels, has contribute disproportionate amounts of carbon dioxide gas into the Earth's atmosphere.
- We now know that more carbon dioxide has been released into the air in the last twenty years *than in all of the centuries before.*
- Knowing that human populations tend to settle near coastlines and in low-lying areas, we can estimate that, at the current rate, tens of millions of people will be displaced by sea rise within the next few decades.
- Reliable estimations are that babies born this year will live to see tens of thousands of South Florida residents flooded out of their homes by the turn of the century.
- We understand that without yearly snow and without glacier and underground aquifer replenishment, there will be no water to spare for irrigation of crops *even though* food production must be increased over the next fifty years to meet the growing population demands.
- We know that neither politicians nor many citizens are willing to make the changes in practice or spend the money required to remedy the situation, *even though the necessary technology is already available.*

- We know that without immediate attention, the catastrophe will be so great that no amount of money could reverse the devastation.

Yet most people are too preoccupied with creature comforts to do anything about it.

Personal note: If you have never read the expeditionary report by Chris Mooney on the Andreas Muenchow and Keith Nicholls journey to Greenland, consider reading it soon. It is well worth your time! It was in the January 1, 2017 issue of *The Washington Post* entitled, "With enough evidence, even the skeptics will thaw." Also, check out this companion video:

http://www.washingtonpost.com/sf/business/2016/12/30/with-enough-evidence-even-skepticism-will-thaw/?utm_term=.26a896e9e2ab

Fresh Water

Some areas of our nation, as indeed, many parts of the world, are running out of fresh water. Legislators choose not to proactively invest the billions needed to prevent that pending disaster. Citizens are not doing enough toward influencing the government as to which battle to pick. With only a few notable exceptions, leaders in government pretend to be unaware of the criticality of looming disastrous situations, and have been unwilling to legislate sorely needed solutions. (Somehow, money always becomes available for disaster relief, but rarely for disaster prevention.)

Many leaders in government have, on the other hand, approved of the transitory benefits oil and gas fracking in the short-term, pursuing a course of action so risky that science can only speculate about a range of consequences in the long-term. Those same leaders are *ignoring* the documented increase of earthquakes, polluted deep-water aquifers, and fouled local wells.

Governments are *approving* companies to build new oil pipelines with the potential of destroying even more freshwater supplies beyond spill recovery. One such section has already broken only two hundred miles from where Native Americans had been demonstrating to warn about exactly such a disaster. Several smaller oil spills have already occurred but were barely reported in the news.

Yet our nation's elected bodies, at all levels of government and without public outcry, have chosen *not* to fix the deteriorating infrastructure of century-old pipes of many towns' water and sewer systems. Moreover, funds that could be invested in correcting deteriorating infrastructure are being misdirected.

For example, the US Army Corps of Engineers and state and local governments are "investing" billions of dollars on hydraulic walls, dykes, barriers and enormous pumps. On top of storm-surge protection, they hope to contain the inevitable encroachment of seawater, which will eventually make swamps out of populated coastal areas. By their actions, leaders in government are asserting if enough money is spent, major rivers and tides can be permanently held back. Yet in some of our aging cities and towns, they cannot even find the necessary funds to assure clean drinking water in public schools right now.

The New Orleans area's colossal pumping stations (when they are operating properly) handle about half of the water in extreme weather events that can lead to massive floods. Could the costs of the pumps and their annual upkeep have been used more effectively to convert fossil fuel—burning electric plants into pollution-free renewable energy?

All this, and we haven't even started to discuss the irrationality of spending billions of dollars on future interplanetary space travel. This in an effort to escape from the mess we have made on Earth. Think how those funds could be better put to use to enhance wind, solar, and perhaps even safe nuclear power sources.

Without citizen involvement and demands, nothing will change.

7: Big Deal #3 - Melting Ice

One fast-changing effect on sea rise is *melting ice*. Don't be misled. Floating icebergs are not a problem. They are in the water and mostly displacing fluid already. Whether from glaciers, ice floes, or frozen tundra, the problem is the melting of ice now on land. When such ice melts, sea levels rise.

In the past twenty-five years, melting of land-based ice has contributed to a sea level rise between three to nine inches in some places around the world. That's a rate of 0.3 inches per year. At that rate, we can expect a rise of up to two feet over the next seventy-five years. If we slow it to *only* 0.2 inches per year, a child born today and living for seventy-five years will see a sea rise of over one foot. The serious unknown is, will the rise hold at 0.2 inches? Or 0.3 inches? Or more? Indications are that the rate is exponentially increasing.

NASA has predicted that under worsening conditions, we may see a sea rise of as much as ten feet in some places over the next century. Consider arithmetically what that means. Imagine the congestion of people, property, or businesses. Consider the low-lying, heavily-populated areas across the world that will be lost to the sea.

This phenomena is changing the face of all land masses. There is a prediction that by 2040, ships will be able to sail over an ice-free North Pole. Sadly, sail without ever seeing a polar bear—by then, likely an extinct species in the wild.

Unmanaged Water Use

We now know that water has been accumulating and replenishing itself in massive aquifers under US Midwest plains for over fifteen thousand years. We know also that humans have pump vast amounts of it out over the past seventy-five years—pumped it to supply water to the country's growing population, and more critically, to irrigate tens of thousands of previously untillable acres for agricultural use.

For a while, scientists thought that the area's aquifers would be replenished naturally from annual melting snows. Left alone, absent unnatural interference, that probably would have happened. However, humans have interfered with natural cycles of both temperature and precipitation, lowering (indeed, practically eliminating) the rate of aquifer replenishment. As a result, aquifer water content has greatly diminished by both direct and indirect means.

It is essential for us to understand that cause-and-effect patterns like these are not a *singular* topic for discussion. Each function in nature directly influences something else. As the first tiny domino is tipped, the chain reaction is set into motion. Without quick and decisive human intervention, the results are inevitable and irreversible. Did you ever see a string of standing dominos "set themselves back up" —or even stopped, without decisive intervention?

Several years ago, while visiting Glacier National Park in Montana, my eighty-year-old guide showed my tour group where vast glaciers used to be. She had been a tour guide at the park for sixty years and told stories that would startle the most jaded skeptic. She swept her arm from the far left to the far right and said, "Once there was nothing but whiteness—nothing but deep snow from one horizon to the other." Then she tried to point out a small snow deposits in a remote valley far away and said, "That's all that's left of that great snow pack." She pointed again to a valley and said, "That once contained one of the great glaciers that made this a national park. Now there isn't enough snow to ski on."

The seasonal melting of these once enormous glaciers supplied drinking water and farm irrigation to millions of people in the states below Montana. Over time, when snow ceases to adequately replenish glaciers, there are no alternative sources for that water. One worried park ranger predicted that the next great civil war will be fought over "water rights." Just imagine fighting your neighbor over a drink of water for your little sister. We are not talking about fighting over water to fill your pool; you may be begging for a sip to survive. This dilemma is already a familiar way of life to tens of thousands of people in many barren and overpopulated regions of the globe. People simply can't imagine such a drought intruding on their comfortable way of life. Consider the following:

- Are you aware that in 2011 alone, 260,000 people starved to death due to drought?
- Did you know that in that same year, 75 percent of *all* livestock in Somalia died of thirst?
- Did you know that those rotting carcasses caused disease and water pollution, which killed thousands more Somali people?
- Can you imagine that *one-third* of the entire world's population already does not have a reliable supply of drinking water?

In 2016, after years of drought, parts of Yosemite National Park received so much snow that the park couldn't open in June. At first glance, one might think, "Great. The West finally gets the water it needs." Continuing to understand the complicated nature of the bigger problem, observe the following sequence:

- Traditionally, the snow pack melts slowly and provides a steady supply of water to the lakes and reservoirs that supply the West.
- This year, the weather was hotter than usual early in the season, causing the snow pack to melt unusually quickly. This resulted in the reservoirs being far too full to handle the volume of water. Millions of gallons of fresh water had to be

released to prevent structural damage to dams, and therefore no longer in reserve for human use. Moreover, sudden releases of huge amounts of water from reservoirs caused unprecedented flooding downstream.

There are nine million people in New York City. If each one flushes the toilet five times a day, and each of those flushes only uses one gallon of fresh water, forty-five million gallons of fresh water are flushed away in one city by one daily process. (No drinking, no bathing, no cooking, no pools.) Multiply that times the entire country of 324 million people, and that's 1.62 billion gallons of fresh water consumed in this country every day just to flush the toilet. Think about what that means. In some parts of the world, children walk miles each day to carry one jug of water home for the family for the day…and that's if there is a well somewhere nearby and the water is not contaminated.

In some parts of the US, the government has already suggested (because there can be no "enforcement") that "If it's yellow, let it mellow." Suggesting that at the very minimum, urine could wait for some accumulation before flushing away a gallon of potable water. I won't ask you how that was accepted in your house.

Heads-up for some Simple Math!

1. In the absence of water restrictions, it is estimated that an average healthy person needs about **thirteen gallons** of water a day for drinking, bathing, and cooking.
2. In many parts of the world, the average use is estimated to be about **five gallons** per day per person—if it can be found and if it is fit to drink.
3. In the United States, according to the US Geological Survey, we average **between eighty and one hundred gallons** of fresh water use per day per person. That's eight to ten times that used by most of the civilized world. We *would* use even more if certain restrictions were not enforced and modern utilities were not so efficiently conservative.

On the other hand, many areas will soon have so much water that parts of the land will be uninhabitable. In an ironic twist of fate, that abundance of water will not be consumable. Rising seas will inundate coastal cities with salt water. Not only will there be insufficient drinking water, but the population will have lost their homes and their businesses, there will be very limited tillable land for farming, and few streets on which to commute. Coasts and inland riverways of many populated countries will be under water during your lifetime.

For example, one entire community on the Ozama River in the Dominican Republic had to be relocated to a public housing development on higher ground in 2017. It is the first of many relocation projects expected by the end of this century caused by rising seas on this island nation.

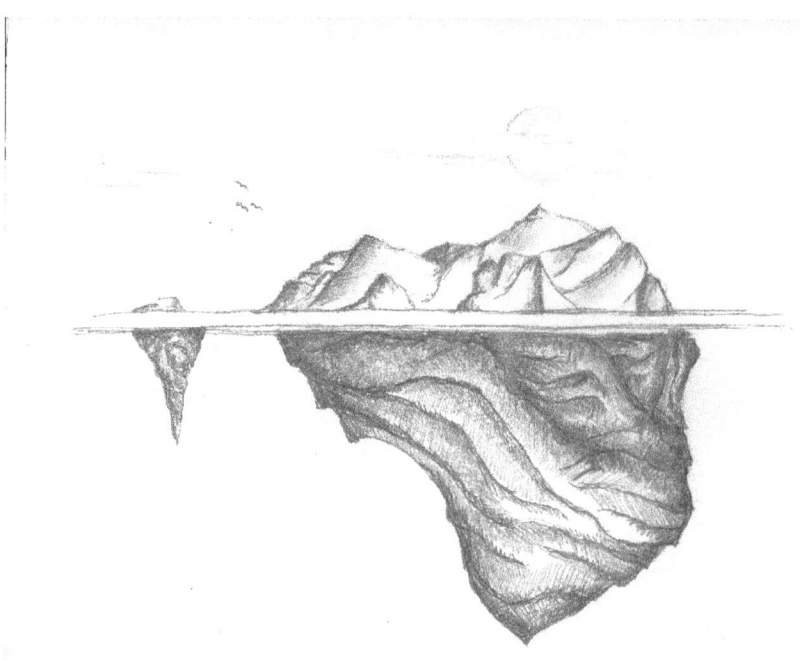

On a trip to Venice, Italy, I once stood in the huge plaza in front of Saint Mark's Basilica, where visitors have been walking on marble sidewalks for fifteen hundred years. Seawater had crept into the plaza, forcing the city to place inverted wooden pallets as walkways to keep tourists' and citizens' feet above several inches of water. Now, just a decade later, there are days when *all* of the shops in the area are inundated with waist-high water. Now they must close their businesses; inventory has been ruined and homes and livelihoods destroyed. The tourism economy is impacted, and perhaps someday, the story of Venice and Saint Mark's will be available only in history books.

Compounding Conditions

There are several regions around the world with widely varied geographic characteristics where the dilemma is especially difficult: sea levels are going up, and at the same time, land itself is going down. In Venice, both land and buildings are slowly sinking due to the natural movement of the tectonic plates on which they were built and the construction methods employed to overcome the swamp-like land on which the buildings were constructed.

Currently, that rate of sinking is as much as one inch per year. Some estimates indicate that the city is already sixteen inches lower than it was the day it was started. The original builders knew that those stone buildings could not be built on mud, swamp, and landfill, so they perfected the art of building on wood pilings driven deep into the seabed. The lack of oxygen kept the poles from rotting, and as a result city survived for over a thousand years. It has long been recognized that the land was sinking, but the movement was exceptionally slow.

Within the last fifty years, however, that pattern has changed drastically. In 2002, an unusually low tide drained Venice's canals so low that gondolas could not operate. Conversely, only six years later, in 2008, standing water in Saint Mark's Square was waist-deep on occasion. The fluctuations are now extreme, and the water table rise is ten times its historic pattern. With the natural lowering of the city's base and the accelerating rise and fluctuation of the surrounding sea levels, Venice, despite massive investment in sea invasion prevention techniques (to buy time,) is *doomed*. At the newly observed increased rate of sinking combined with rising sea levels, parts of the city may have to be abandoned by as early as 2030.

Recall our discussion on the thermal expansion of the oceans. Observe that this phenomenon, caused by warming waters, contributes to the sheer volume of water in the ocean. That added volume seeks relief in low-lying coastal towns and below sea-level depressions, the very areas where many people live and work.

Conversely, due to consequences of overpopulation in Florida, tens of thousands of wells are extracting water out of freshwater aquifers beneath homes and offices. The results of that are twofold:

First, water customarily seeped through the sand quite slowly, making its way from the sea to the aquifer. As it moved, it was filtered—rural residents refer to this as *percolating*. With high demand leading to the rapid removal of water from aquifers, the slow filtering process can no longer take place. Either the ground (previously pure sand) is saturated with salt leached from the salt water as it passes through, or the speed of the draw is too fast for the percolation to occur (or both).

Second, the previously saturated ground of the peninsula of Florida was balanced. Now, pumping is removing water from in and under the earth at a comparatively fast pace. Dry earth shrinks significantly. Empty aquifers create cavities. As a result of these and other factors, some state residents are now facing sinkholes that consume houses and cars, and are, in some cases, far too large to fill. Some land cannot be reclaimed.

All of these are simple examples of repercussions that arise when nature is knocked out of balance by human interference on a grand scale. While somewhat different, the extraction of underground gas and oil (and even water) in other parts of the country are causing similar irreparable destruction. I urge you to investigate the unnerving relationship between fracking and earthquakes.

In Florida, in contrast to Venice, we have salt contamination of the sand that feeds freshwater aquifers as well as the rise of sea levels on all sides of the peninsula. The loss to the economy is going to be staggering as homes, businesses, and the tourism industry are all overtaken by salt water. It's not that property values will fall—it's that ultimately there will be no property to sell.

Melting Glaciers

In most cases, the situation is worse than it appears to the eye. Polar glaciers are melting from the top *and* (studies now prove) from the bottom.

As contaminants in the air (some from the domestic and industrial pollution of humans and some from the sediment from naturally occurring volcanic eruptions) settle on the once pure white surface of great ice masses, the glaciers accumulate a blanket of dark particles. Previously, the glossy-white surfaces have reflected the heat of the sun and simply added to a slick, hard cover protecting to the snow and ice below. Now, with surfaces becoming a gray-black, dingy blanket, the heat of the sun is readily absorbed, analogous to the dark background of a modern solar panel.

The sun's heat is absorbed and melts the top layer until the ice is warmed to a flowing stream of water, seeking every crack and fissure through which to escape. The fast-running water erodes deep chasms in the body of ice and carries the warm water deep into the ice bed.

You probably would not notice much difference in the (now discolored) top layer of ice, visible from the air and even from a land-based observation point. However, careful inspection shows that the warming surface (mostly due to heat absorption caused by a *lack* of the sun's reflection) now allows this sun-warmed water to flow *through* cracks in the glaciers, down *under* the bottoms of the mass. This surface-warmed water now raises the temperature of previously protected waters *under* the ice. Warmed water laps erosively at the bottom of the glaciers before it flows on into the once iced-in rivers. That erosion, which thins and weakens the bottoms of these formations, is not visible until the top slab gets so thin that it cracks apart, allowing immense portions to break off and float out to sea.

As explained previously, icebergs currently floating anywhere in the sea will not measurably raise the sea levels when they melt. They are already displacing area by floating in the water. The 10 to 20 percent of icebergs showing above the waterline will not be that dangerous. The massive ice cover on *land*, which is rapidly melting from consequences of air pollutants and heat, will indeed raise sea levels. Estimates vary, but (depending on the area) levels may rise between two and ten feet in the next fifty years—either number is shocking. If we idly sit by and watch that happen, tens of millions of people living in the most populated cities in the world will be forces to relocate. Unless steps are taken, rising seas will inundate millions of square miles of inhabited land, and there will not be sufficient fresh water to support people's lifestyles. The loss of homes and lives will be exacerbated by the loss of businesses and jobs.

According to a nonprofit group called the Union of Concerned Scientists, using the past fifty years as a basis, in the United States:

- the West Coast has experienced a sea level rise of two to four inches;
- the East Coast is up six inches in Boston, seven inches in New York City, and ten inches in Norfolk;
- Miami is actually raising the surface of their roads to accommodate daily inundation by high tides, *and*
- Gulf Coast cities like Galveston, Texas, have already seen a recorded rise of twelve inches.

Can you imagine the social turmoil and human devastation that this will bring?
Neighbor against neighbor, town against town...
the impact is unthinkable.

Complicated, Interrelated Balance

In a recent trip to Yosemite National Park in California, we pulled up to our cabin, and my first question to the receptionist was, "What happened to your trees?" On the drive in, we could not avoid noticing that one-third to one-half of the impressively tall pine trees on mountainsides in all directions had died. The dead trees were comingled among those still hanging on to life. We were at about four thousand feet above sea level.

In discussion with the elderly owner, who was a lifelong resident, we were told:

1. For five years, there had been little to no rain or snow and that the forty- and fifty-year-old trees were all in distress, making them weak and vulnerable.
2. Bark beetles had infested the entire forest, and weaker trees succumbed to the destructive beetles.
3. Stronger, healthy, well-nourished trees can fight off the annual devastation caused by invasive beetles, but weakened ones cannot.
4. Additionally and equally critical: each year, typical cold, winter weather kills millions of beetles and their larva, thereby helping to control the beetle population. With warmer winters of recent years, however, the proliferation of this beetle population has gone unchecked.
5. When the spring invasions of beetles overwhelms weakened trees, the trees inevitably die.

Bark beetles attack pine, fir, cedar, and spruce trees, among others, particularly those weakened by drought and environmental stress. It is estimated millions of trees in western North America have died due to bark beetle infestations in only the past decade.

Undeniable Proof

We continued the drive up to six thousand feet above sea level and beyond. Based on the owner's characterization, we expected to find still more newly dead trees. But at seven thousand feet, we observed that the mountains are beautifully green, thickly populated with conifers of all kinds. There was only an occasional dead tree. At eight thousand feet, there were virtually no dead trees.

The logic is elementary, as is so much of the problem and the solution. *First,* in the higher elevations, warming in the park has not yet completely unbalanced the amount of snow and rain received.

The well-nourished trees are strong, healthy, and able to fight off the invasive beetles. *Second*, cold winters at higher elevations have continued to kill off the beetles each winter and—at the very least—kept the population of these harmful pests in check.

Such observable examples are everywhere. The logic of the dead trees is not that difficult to understand. It is our responsibility to explain these fundamentals to everyone. As we have discussed before, the elected legislators who control the use of the public funds will do nothing without pressure from the voters.

Is the public unaware of the power it has? Is the public unaware of the need for immediate involvement, and is the public too complacent to make a call or write a letter? (Yes, I mean a *letter*—not an email!)

8: A Call for Action

The first and most critical step toward eliminating global warming is getting citizens informed and involved. Moving any government to action requires an overwhelming demand from knowledgeable constituents.

Good decision-making must be forced by *this* generation of young people, and that skill must be mastered quickly. While older adults fantasize about space travel and pretend they can contain the Mississippi, young people have some critical thinking to do. This generation has life-and-death discussions to make here on Earth—here, and right now. Their decisions must be made based on proven facts, without emotion, without politics, and without short-sightedness. Their work is beyond urgent. It has become critical. There is a disaster to be prevented, and there's no time for self-serving opinions, irrational emotions, or dangerous procrastination. *Decisions are currently being made based on the unprecedented denial of facts and patterns.* The continued misrepresentation of facts must stop immediately!

There is nothing disrespectful about rethinking past generations' beliefs.
We understand that many of them simply didn't know any better.
This is not new.
We must remember that throughout history,
educated and religious people insisted that,
"The world is flat."

Now, we *do* know better about the world's warming and changing climate. It was once difficult for informed people to understand why climate change skeptics—with all the accumulated data—continue to debate the existence, not to mention the urgency, of the problem. Now, it has become far more serious than difficult to understand. As we have discussed, we are simply out of time. They, and sometimes we, choose to ignore the urgency and the inevitability of the consequences of inaction.

That responsibility shouldn't be hard to understand, yet it seems to be. Young people of this generation are now faced with a situation like none other. In 1945, the United States' decision to drop an atomic bomb on Hiroshima, Japan was made knowing that tens of *thousands* of innocent civilians would die. By 2045, we may be measuring casualties in the *millions*.

Fifty years ago, the US spent $19 billion in a race against the Soviet Union to put a "man on the moon." Can you imagine where we would be if we had spent that much money and talent on the development of renewable energy alternatives? Nay-sayers often claim that America is wasting its time and money on such matters while nations in Asia and Africa do little. Perhaps the US role could be to perfect affordable technologies, solve our own problem, and then market it to developing countries. Talk about Made in America "job creation."

Keep in perspective that
this generation of Mars-chasing adults
<u>will be long gone when it's too late</u>.
They will never experience the horrors of a doomsday,
a global famine,
or a civil war over water.
However, today's children and their grandchildren <u>will</u> be here.
It is their existence and their survival as a species that is at stake.

This is now far past "inconvenient."
No more time for denial.
No more time for debating.
No more time for resistance.

Since young people have the most at stake and the most to lose, they must be encouraged to think through and discuss the issues with fresh, open minds and youthful energy. They will need the support of citizens at every level and every legislative bodies they elect. They must develop and execute a comprehensive plan to resolve this quandary. If they fail…

*Who among us will be on stage
when the curtain goes down
on the final act of this tragic play?*

The pain of starvation, the fear of a tsunami-like tides, the horror of civil disobedience, disease, and massive unemployment are all real possibilities.

They are so unthinkable that many well-meaning, sophisticated people refuse to dare think about them. Refusing to face these possibility is exactly why the problem hasn't been adequately addressed.

This generation, acting as a part of the unselfish, informed, and energetic generation that I know you to be, have a great deal to accomplish and precious little time in which to do it. Self-serving politicians and antiscience zealots must not threaten you. You must educate yourself…. You must educate them. Your attention must not be diverted by their misguided beliefs and propaganda. You specifically must not be dissuaded by claims of "high costs" or "unavailable funds."

Find the money! Make the hard choices needed to focus on Earth's survival. If that's not enough, even though you understand the real need for social program spending, and maybe even the desire for space travel, allocate and redirect that spending! If that's not enough, impose new survival taxes, and create new business incentives toward clean energy production. You must find the money *now*, or you will never need money again.

You must do this because, putting it bluntly:

- There is no social program big enough to help a billion people standing knee-deep in water.
- There is no social program big enough to feed and house seven billion people.
- There is no escape through space travel unless there are people in base-camps on Earth to support it.

Today, our government is still having a difficult time helping citizens recover from one hurricane that happened over a decade ago. How effectively do you think it will respond to universal flooding, starvation, civil disobedience, and plague? Even if any government finally gets better organized in response to the crisis, where will the money come from if there are not enough people working to pay sufficient taxes?

> *Let's get more specific and more serious about exactly what you must do.*

Make no mistake! You are now in a life-or-death situation. This is not about party politics or budgetary considerations. You are talking about the environment of the planet you live on being destroyed in exchange for near-term gratification. Understand that Planet Earth will be here for a long, long time—spinning unfailingly around the sun—with or without humanity. It may not have any people living on it at the comfort levels we now enjoy. There may be acidic lakes and oceans, barren mountains, deserts and ice caps, and perhaps even some lower forms of life.

> *Humankind may have to start all over. Who knows, maybe next time we'll get it right.*

We have forced onto your shoulders a situation to which only your generation can provide the remedy. It has now fallen to you to:

- acquire the **wisdom**, integrity, and deep understanding of the situation;
- develop a last-chance plan—as if **money** for the solution were no object;
- develop political, technical, and project **management skills** to implement the plan;
- educate all people to reach a common **acceptance** and level of understanding that makes it a universally accepted plan (this is far beyond an American problem);
- discover **technical alternatives and methods** required to eliminate the problems **at their origin;**
- understand the **urgency** and criticality of your limited time;
- understand the incredibly **complicated interrelationships** of the selling the tasks ahead of you and yet the **simplicity of the solution**; and finally,
- find, develop, and bolster the **political will** and public support you need to implement your plan.

These are only a few bulleted ideas for you to consider. You will expand and improve the list as your understanding grows. These tasks are doable. The causes are known—even self-evident. You must increase and develop this comprehensive list of problems by observing, identifying, and recording every detail of what's happening. That comprehensive list of issues will direct your path to plan for a solution. You must do this methodically because, as Charles Kettering said:

"A problem well stated is a problem half solved."

Please don't gloss over Kettering's words. Reflect a moment on that statement. Your work *is* truly half-finished when the problem statement is well-defined. Your well-informed generation, when shown exactly what needs to be done, will have the framework of your remediation plan.

Our problem has been that there are too few individuals with the courage to buck the system. There are not enough Al Gores (look at what costs he paid). It's time for you and your friends to first identify and understand the problem, and then work knowing that Mother Nature is depending on you to save her. Remember:

- **Wisdom** is that basic acceptance and understanding of valid and reliable facts, supported by that ability to recognize cause-and-effect relationships, and intuiting *what to do with that data and information* ... all of it, polished by experience.
- **Money** always seems to be the first fundamental problem to solve before you can even start on the correction process. However, you will never generate enough money without being able to explain the criticality of the situation to the masses.
- **Jobs**, predicted by critics to be lost, will be replaced by alternative-energy jobs. Tens of thousands of jobs at all levels will be needed to design, build, install, and maintain wind turbines and solar panels as well as in land and water management.

If you wait, as is the traditional way of addressing most issues, there will be few buildings in which to have a debate, no need for an angry mob to protest, and no press to print the newspaper and no money, when so much is underwater or consumed by uncontrollable drought-driven fires.

At the risk of being redundant: there *is* money. Funds can be redirected from projects that will hardly matter fifty years from now when rising seas have extensively reshaped existing shorelines.

Just watch: things that are worshipped, debated, and funded today, perceived by many to be important, will all become irrelevant!

Unfortunately, it will be too late to reopen the dialogue.
"I told you so!" or "I'm sorry!" will do nothing.

You cannot allow yourselves to be dissuaded by poorly informed climate change skeptics asserting unscientific propaganda. You cannot because there simply isn't any time left for you to negotiate with them, explain it to them, or to ask their permission. The air you breathe, the food you eat, the water you drink, and the weather in which you survive are all fading fast. The seasons, the tides, the temperatures, the sea levels, and the very environment that you have come to know as natural is being taken away from you at an alarming and exponential rate, and taken away forever.

*****

What Can I Do?

Now that you have a better idea of the dilemma and its complicated, potentially disastrous results, it's time to ask, "What can I do?" Indeed, it may be more essential to ask, "What *must* I do?" because it has now fallen to you and your generation to reverse the path we are on, the path from complacency to destruction:

1. *Read. Study. Learn. Act.* Become a subject matter expert on climate change and the repercussions of global warming. Even then, you may be faced with underinformed skeptics. Some doubters are malicious and have self-serving reasons behind their attempts to avoid the reality; some are uninformed or unconvinced, and some are unaccustomed to the depth of thinking required.
2. Insist—indeed, demand—that your community's schools and colleges offer you the technical tools and skills you will need to fight this battle. Take advantage of those offerings. You will need a wide breadth of understanding to change the minds of skeptics.
3. Become a grassroots organizer. You can't do this alone. This must not be your final crusade. (The survival of our culture will be your reward.)

4. Unite your voice with others to constructively challenge your legislators at every level of government. You'll need to be articulate, knowledgeable, wise, and relentless.
5. Become politically active. Be an educator, a scientist, or an elected official advocating for education and legislation to combat climate change.
6. Generate and maintain an enthusiasm and energy you didn't know you had, and don't be dissuaded by those fighting for the status quo.
7. Close this book, take a deep breath, and inhale the fresh air with the authority and responsibility your understanding has brought you. Check out your image in the mirror, display the biggest smile of confidence you have ever mustered, and say aloud:

"I've got this!"

Let's Put this Conversation in Perspective

Simply put, nature is not a thing. It is not singularly the wind or air, water, plants, or animals; there is not anything you can put on a list to stand alone to represent all of nature. There is no one thing that can be changed to solve the bigger problem. This is a complex scenario, and it must be understood as a whole.

Not so simply put, nature is life's creation itself. It is the most delicately integrated, complicated, and (note this next word!) *balanced* system ever in existence. Nature is a most codependent group of interrelated systems that has evolved over millions of years. In the last 125 years, humankind has at first unknowingly and today consciously managed to foul up that balance! We have interfered with the very *balance* and the *sequence* that has sustained this magnificently beautiful planet for eons.

9: Final Thoughts

We are approaching a tipping point, a moment that may lead to irreversible changes around the world. It's a point never before faced in the history of civilization; a point so critical to the survival of humankind that the damage may be irreversible. It will be the day on which legislators and the citizens who voted for them—those who have been unwilling to accept the science before them—ask each other, "How did we let this happen?"

Those who have studied and understand the imminent and irreparable dangers are sometimes accused of being *dystopian*—an imagined place or state in which everything is unpleasant. Would you call residents who leave town because a tornado is on the horizon dystopian? Of course not, because:

- Their fear is not imagined.
- They have been warned.
- Their desire for self-preservation is the first law of nature.
- Their past experience indicates immediate action is required.

These fundamental decisions are made by thinking people based on information and experience. Why then is the world's changing climate so different?

As we grow and our brains develop, we move from primitive instinctive and involuntary actions to conscious thought and behavior. We all follow a fundamental pattern of learning:

- We pick up pieces of *data*—and we call them numbers, letters, sounds, and symbols. Standing alone, detached from one another, they mean little, but they are the foundation of our intellect.
- We combine these pieces of data into *information*—and we call them words, formulae, sentences, and eventually thoughts. We see the beginnings of cause-and-effect behavior, such as how the word *cookie* and a smile yield results in young children.
- Almost everyone goes on to learn to group information into *knowledge*. They *know* how to communicate and to tell you how to bake a cake, grow a melon, or build a boat. However…

Far too few make the last transition of turning knowledge into *wisdom*. Some seem incapable, but most are simply unwilling. It is at the point when people can digest a thought or sequence a story and can fully comprehend the repercussions of every tiny detail before making a decision. At this point, they can understand cause-and-effect relationships and the meaning and power of every word they speak. Unless and until people understand the depth and complications of life as we know it, only then they may get deeply involved with the critical topic at hand.

> When you know *what to do with*
> the knowledge you have accumulated,
> then you have obtained wisdom.

We now have all of the data, information, and knowledge about global warming that we can ever possibly need or use. Who among us has the wisdom to act on that accumulation of knowledge?

If we keep ignoring the truth about global warming; if we're going to continue doing the same things we have been doing for the past seventy-five years, and if we continue to *live only for today*, then indeed, one day in the not-too-distant future, people will wake up, look out of their windows, and realize that it's too late.

*****

*That generation will have finally found the answer
to the unthinkable question;
All humanity will come to the grim realization that they are,
in fact,
going to be
The Last Generation.*

About the Graphic Artist

Philip Taylor graduated from the Rochester Institute of Technology shortly after the end of the last glaciation period in the northern hemisphere. He has lived and worked as a graphic designer in San Diego since seeking out warmer climates and has few, if any, regrets. He and his wife Pamela have two children, Ian and Sarah. In addition to art and design, Philip's other interests include woodworking, amateur chefery, reading, cosmology, and volleyball (both watching and playing).

For inquires, contact Philip at taylor.philip@att.net.

About the Author

Thom Shipley comes to professional writing after several careers in which his technical and informative writing skills were honed. His credentials as an educator have been gathered from firsthand experience and education at the University of Maryland, Loyola University, Nova University, and many graduate programs and advanced studies.

Thom's first professional career as an educator started in Anne Arundel County, Maryland, and ranged from being the first elementary instrumental music instructor on an eleven-school circuit to the high school band director and head of a well-respected music department at his alma mater, Glen Burnie High School. Thom was called to be vice principal of the prestigious Severna Park High School; from there, he was promoted to become the first Coordinator of Educational Information Systems for the Anne Arundel County School System. After several years in Annapolis, his groundbreaking work in the application of information technology to curriculum and administrative processes was recognized by his being selected to be the first chief information officer for the Maryland State Department of Education. At the time of his retirement after thirty-one years of service, he was acting as an assistant superintendent of schools for business and finance for the Maryland State Department of Education.

Three days after retiring from the State Department of Education, Thom was recruited to start his second career by accepting a position on Capitol Hill as the executive director of the National Association of Federally Impacted Schools, a new association of public schools dealing with federal funding for American Indian and military-dependent students. While there, he also became a consultant to the House and Senate subcommittees on education. After growing that organization from thirty districts to over six hundred districts and from $400 million to $1.4 billion, he retired in 1988 to become a serial entrepreneur.

Later, Thom went to work for Kaiser Permanente. For the next twelve years, he was the care delivery liaison between the medical and administrative staffs at thirty-two medical facilities and the organization's information technology department. He retired from Kaiser Permanente in 2012 to try his hand at writing. He also counsels budding entrepreneurs at the University of Baltimore's School of Business and was recently recognized as mentor of the year by the Small Business Administration's SCORE organization.

Thom and his partner, Chris, have completed the restoration and decoration of a three-story Victorian row home in the cultural center of Baltimore's midtown district. They are active with the city's orchestra, live-performances theaters, a college lecture series, a chorus, and travel.

Thom has published books titled *Pop's Short Stories* and *The Revitalization of the American Classroom*. All books are available for purchase on amazon.com or thomshipleybooks.com. He is also working on another book of short stories that reflects his eye-opening life experiences during the racial transitions of the 1940s and 1950s.

You may reach him at his website:
www.thomshipleybooks.com.

www.ingramcontent.com/pod-product-compliance
Lightning Source LLC
Chambersburg PA
CBHW071109030426
42336CB00013BA/2014